NV 509

MARY OF NAZARETH

MARY
of Nazareth

by

Igino Giordani

Translated

by

Mother Clelia Maranzana, R.C.

AND

Mother Mary Paula Williamson, R.C.

ST. PAUL EDITIONS

Nihil obstat
    John M. A. Fearns, S.T.D.
                    Censor Librorum.

Imprimatur
    ✠ Francis Cardinal Spellman
            Archbishop of New York.

Library of Congress Catalog Card Number: 65-24079

Printed in U.S.A. by the *Daughters of St. Paul*
50 St. Paul's Ave., Jamaica Plain, Boston, Mass. 02130

FOREWORD

A book on our Lord's mother is always timely; but never more timely than in these bedeviled days. For, the sick sad world, stupefied from the long glut of matter, quantity, speed and pleasure, has wanton-like been quenching the lights that should guide its faltering feet, and one of those quenched lights is, tragically enough, the Christian ideal of womanhood: the ideal for which the Church has done age-long battle. For the Catholic Church has always enshrined in honor the valiant woman who, looking to God's mother as her life's pattern, sweetens the home, inspires reverence, refines manners, restrains frivolity, shames away impurity, teaches self-respect and self-sacrifice, devotion and patience, and sheds around her the sweet fragrance of modesty and chastity.

But just as surely as modern men and women have moved away from this Christian ideal, just so surely have they moved in the direction of barbarism and have thereby contributed one of the most destructive elements to the "revolution of destruction" which imperils the world to-day and which will shatter the fabric of civilized society unless countered with the power of the Madonna's virtues.

The descent into barbarism cannot be mistaken. The courts of divorce, the ubiquitous sexy advertisements, the shady stage and film, the prurient novel with its seared "heroines," the pagan "beauty contests" and the sordid romances that make big news in the daily press—all these spread before our eyes a picture of womanhood that is poles apart from the Christian ideal, and reveals, to an alarming degree, the disease of a society that knows not the Virgin Mother and the Christ to whom she leads men.

In the face of such a gloomy prospect, the appearance of Igino Giordani's *Mary of Nazareth: a true portrait*, and its translation into English prepared by two Religious of the Cenacle, must be welcomed with gratitude and joy. In this fascinating story, so beautifully told, the Mother of Jesus is made to live again among us in the fulness of God's grace and in the charm of her womanly virtues in order that "she may offer an ideal to a generation torn by war." Such is the author's underlying purpose. He has touchingly dedicated his book to the mother of his children. That alone is a call to other men to enthrone Mary as Queen in their households to sanctify them.

In *Mary of Nazareth* we follow God's spotless Mother from the moment she received the Archangel's tremendous message at Nazareth, to the moment of her bodily passage into glory. Thereafter, we follow her through history and see her grow in the love of men. They carry her sweet name to the shores of America in the *Santa Maria* of Columbus, to spread it over forest and prairie. She is the inspiration of poets and sages, of sculptors and painters, of theologians and orators— God's fairest creature untouched by sin. Hence every title of honor belongs to her and human language is inadequate to phrase them all.

But, Giordani insists, Mary is not just an historic memory. She still abides with us at a time when her help is most needed. She is with us by the power of her example and by the grace she wins for men through her mediation. She is reflected in chaste wives and pure virgins who "in the midst of the muddy flood of wantonness and of avarice" are "like many filters of purification."

That Mary may be similarly reflected in every man and woman who reads this inspiring book, and that the readers of it may be numerous beyond count, is the fondest wish of both author and translators. They would ask for no greater reward. May they receive it in good measure.

Demetrius B. Zema, S.J.

Auriesville, N. Y.

TRANSLATOR'S NOTE

The author of this book, Igino Giordani, claims it as his favorite among the numerous volumes that have come from his pen. This is understandable. Solid and intelligent piety needs Mary, the Mother of Jesus, loves her and seeks her aid. Not a day passes but sincere Catholics pay homage to Mary of Nazareth because of her immense dignity as Mother of the Redeemer and of the redeemed.

American Catholics, especially, need this book by Igino Giordani. *Mary of Nazareth* may be described as a contemplation of the Blessed Virgin; a meditation according to the Ignation method; an epic poem in prose; and lastly, the written testimony of one who loves the Madonna tenderly and ardently, and has told her story with all the artistry of a poet.

CLELIA MARANZANA R.C.
MARY PAULA WILLIAMSON R.C.

Boston, Mass.

Usual abbreviations:

A.H. Analecta Hymnica medii sevi.
                         Dreves, Leipzig; 1886

P.G. Patrologia Greaca (Migne)

P.L. Patrologia Latina (Migne)

The New Testament as translated by Monsignor Ronald Knox, Sheed and Ward, New York, 1944

PREFACE

The Virgin Proclaimed

De Maria numquam satis: Never enough is said of Mary. This saying of theologians and scholars gives the author his purpose for writing this book. In fact, it is almost unavoidable not to speak or write of the Madonna, because, as St. Germanus says, "She is the very breath of the baptized soul; the air in which we live and move. We cannot do without her."

"Do you wish to know God?" ask the sacred writers. "Read Mary as a book."

"Do you wish to know Christ? Then study Mary."

"If Christ is the sun, then Mary is the sky; if Christ is the gem, then Mary is the jewel case. If Christ is the sun, Mary is the plant." [1]

The desire to speak of her has been the inspiration of these pages, and they are offered as a small tribute of praise, a tribute which turned out to be a story about her. The desire to speak of her under certain aspects has resulted in a synthesis on her maternity. In a strict sense, and humanly speaking, the historical sources for knowledge about her, are very few— the Gospels. The rest belongs to apocryphal literature, and ordinarily one does not make use of this, out of reverence for the subject. The sources, then, are scanty enough. She is our Mother, and that is sufficient for children who love her, delight in being near her, hearing her and knowing her; they need no other biographical data.

In fact, nascent Christianity experienced so much pleasure

---

[1] Hysychius, P.G. 63, 1465.

in the refuge of her arms that no care or concern was taken to preserve facts which would have been required for one detached and distant, rather than for one so loved and always so near. Nevertheless, one cannot reduce the life of Mary of Nazareth to a series of humble incidents happening in that small border region of Palestine in the time of Augustus and Tiberius Caesar; for those incidents four or five pages would suffice.

The truth is that the story of Mary begins in Eternity and continues on without interruption. It is the story of a miracle, God, the Lover-Creator, wrought for His own joy and that of the whole world. To speak of her is to present her in her marvelous quality, a creature upon whom God has lavished His glorious essence of grace: she is a being placed midway between the Godhead and man, between the past and the future, between life and death. She is a creature who became the mother of the Creator; who being mortal gave flesh to God. By an infinite miracle, she was made the instrument for inserting the Word of God into humanity.

St. Mechtilde describes Mary as a microcosm, "a miniature world," in the creation of which, God took more infinite care than He did in creating the universe. Her story is, therefore, bound up with the perennial fact of the continuous reconciliation of mankind with God, and it is also bound up with the eternal glory of Christ her Son. She is an immense cycle which would bewilder any man, but the writer has done his best; certainly it is very little. He has not forced the subject, even though his pen has moved swiftly, almost of itself. If he has not said more, nor in a better manner, it is because he has not known how to do so.

It is because of what the author himself has discovered about the Madonna in the writing of this book, that he dedicates it to the mother of his own children. This is obvious, since in a Christian home, the mother and the wife are a feeble image of the Church and of Mary, because from the Church we ascend to Mary.

For the theological part which reaches sublime mysteries in the spiritual life, the manuscript has been thoroughly examined by a competent and accurate theologian, Reverend Father Gabriel M. Roschini of the Order of Servites, who took upon himself this task out of love for her whose servant he is. For this service to me, I thank him.

If, after all this explanation, the author speaks so feebly of the ALL PURE, he may be allowed to offer the same excuses as those who lived in the days so much nearer to her. That theologian, the great lover of the Virgin Mary, who lived in the East, St. John Damascene, used to say: "It is not that she needs our praises but *we* need *her glory*." [2] That is it, we need her glory.[2] In making her known, the one most marvelous, we simply fulfill a necessity of life. He also said, "When we praise her, we pay a debt, so that towards her we are forever indebted." [3] Thus he addressed her, "O daughter Empress Queen, accept this prayer from a sinful slave who loves you. With reason do all generations call you *Blessed!* You are the chosen glory of humanity."

That other knight of our Lady, in the West, St. Bernard of Clairvaux wishing to carry out a project (which had often come to his mind) to say something in praise of the Virgin Mary, and feeling his incapacity, begged her thus, "Do not, O Mother of the Word Incarnate, despise my petitions." Again he exclaims, "Nothing so delights me, and yet nothing so frightens me, as to speak of the glories of Mary." [4]

Petrarch expresses a similar sentiment in verse, drawn to poetry by his love for woman, then rising to the greater height of his love for the Madonna:

---

[2] In Dormitatione B.V. Mariae III L; P.G. 96, 753.
[3] St. John Damascene, op. cit. I, II; P.G. 96, 680.
[4] Preface to the homilies on *Missus est,* P.L. 183, 55.

"O Virgin fair, clothed with the sun [5]
and crowned with the stars,
In thee the Supreme Sun was pleased to
hide His light."
Love moves me to speak these
words of thee.

Therefore, whoever dares to write of her is drawn to do so by a compelling love. At any rate, he may shelter himself under the words of another great Mother of the Church— St. Gertrude, who prayed thus: "Lord, since You became Man and our Brother, to supply for all our defects, I beg of You that You deign likewise, to supply for all my defects in worthily praising the Most Blessed Virgin, Thy Mother." [6]

What better ideal and hope could be offered to our generation so torn by war, than the Divine Motherhood of Mary which is capable of awakening in us the sense of our supernatural brotherhood, thanks to Christ her son and our brother?

IGINO GIORDANI

---

[5] *Canzone alla Vergine*, 7, 4.
[6] St. Gertrude, "Revelations," Chs. III, IV.

CONTENTS

2. *Nazareth*

Chapter V
THE MOTHER OF THE FAMILY

Chapter VI
THE CO-REDEMPTRIX

Chapter VII
MOTHER OF THE CHURCH

Chapter VIII
THE GATE AND WINDOW OF HEAVEN

Chapter IX
THE VIRGIN MOTHER OF POETRY

Chapter X
MOTHER OF GOD AND MOTHER OF MEN

A Virgin

Shall Conceive

The dew of Heaven
And the flower of the field
We received from thee,
Sweet Mary.

A new light,
And a true God,
We adore, through thee
Holy Mary.[1]

IN THE DAYS OF HEROD

Herod, the King of Judea, was now laden with years and
with crimes. The crimes did not weigh heavily upon him,
but the years did. If at times his glance swept over to the
barren mountains of his realm from the fortress of Machaerus,
or from the Herodiun, he was not remembering his many
massacres but the edifices he had built and his military
achievements. Much astuteness had been necessary to keep his
throne, continually menaced as he was by Roman suspicion
towards the Jews, and then by the Jews who despised strangers, particularly the Romans.

In his royal apartments nine wives wandered about. They
were of two types, like gazelles or like tigresses. He had already killed one, named Mariamne, and she was the one he
loved most. In her blood and in her features she bore the like-
ness of the Hasmoneans. It was in the service of the Has-
monean dynasty that Herod, his brother and his father, had

---

[1] Coeli rorem
Campi florem
Ex te accepimus
Duleis Maria

Novum lumen,
Verum numen
Per te adoramus
Santa Maria

A.H. VIII, 78,6.

all three carried arms and fought. In fact they had fought so well and so cleverly that kings had been overthrown, their sons and other relations killed, and now they had taken their places.

When Herod, dragging himself with fatigue up and down the largest terrace of the Machaerus, thought of all this, he gnashed his teeth with rage and, with a gesture of his hand, seemed to drive away the ghosts of all the princes whom he had butchered.

All his wives, with their daughters and sons—his sons— were like a brood of vipers who might scheme to poison him by dark plots. Were it not for his giant Galatian guard, who did not understand the language of his household, Herod could never feel safe, even in the midst of his own family. His sons brought him few joys, for they inherited the art of intrigue from their mothers and the art of homicide from him, but inherited none of his talents.

His daughter Salome was involved with Augustus in Rome, while her sisters were plotting against her in Judea. His son Antipater had already gone to Rome to secure support for himself from the court and the assurance of his succession to the throne when the old man died.

At the mere thought of death Herod was always seized with a blind fury in which he would have done away with his own flesh and blood, destroying the succession as if that could ward off the hour of his death, and also put an end to family quarrels. Once he had loved his own people. He had desired children and he often found himself sighing for one of his little ones looking up at him with innocent eyes and taking tiny steps, but now he was old and suffering from gout. The little ones might have helped him forget his years and have given him a sense of beginning life anew.

In Rome his royal master Augustus was also strolling through the avenues of the Palatine. He stopped to gaze at the city spread out at his feet watered by the Tiber that went its winding way with the glow and tints of the setting sun playing upon it. He, too, recalled the massacres by which he had reduced to peace the people of Rome and subdued them in the bondage of the city. The Senate flattered him by erecting a fine altar called purposely "Peace." The Temple of Janus was closed because wars were ended and there was now peace.

Peace, however, was lacking to Augustus. His wife and daughter were heaping shame on the glory of his name by the vile deeds to which they abandoned themselves and the intrigues in which they involved him. He had been obliged to isolate his daughter on an island, and he lived in continual fear of his wife. His home was now empty of children, and his son Marcellus, a child prodigy, sung by the poets, the hope of his father and of Rome, had died. Marcellus had been strong, beautiful and intelligent. It was said that he had been snatched away by the gods—or *was* it by the gods? Remembering this child at the sunset hour made Augustus feel the heavy weight of his years and gave him the impression that the whole world was growing old. The world, too, crudely felt the need of a Divine Child Who could restore to it its youth and peace.

Virgil, the poet—he, too, was dead—had foretold the coming of a boy with whom a new order of things would begin. The Persians had awaited this child; also the Medes, and other peoples farther away. The world was becoming old and decayed, its sunset was tinted with blood while it looked for the budding of a Divine Infant Who would bring the pure light of a new day.

ZACHARY AND ELIZABETH

The same thought of a childless old age—like a sunset that faded into darkness without the hope of returning dawn—

also haunted Zachary, a priest of Judea, and his wife Elizabeth. Old age had overtaken them in a solitary mountain village and, with the years, their sadness had increased. To them
childlessness was like a condemnation of God. With deep
humility they had continually implored God the Father and
Creator of all who are born, to grant them the gift of offspring. They asked this for their own consolation and to end
their humiliation in appearing before the world like two
barren tree trunks blighted by the Most High God.

On a day preceding the Sabbath, Zachary left the village
early in the morning to go to Jerusalem and to fulfill there
his priestly duties in the Temple; duties of which he was an
exact and jealous observer. He was a descendant of Aaron, as
was also his wife Elizabeth; both were irreproachable and always mindful of their priestly dignity, even in their poverty.
That week it was the turn of Zachary's class—that of Abias,
the eighth of the twenty-four classes of priests—to direct the
many ceremonies in the Temple.

He walked along the country road full of puddles and
clumps of mud washed down from the slopes by the early
rains and, looking ahead of him in the pale light of dawn, the
Temple seemed to rise before him like a mountain of snow:
the great Temple of Jerusalem which Herod had rebuilt.
Zachary, with the other priests had helped to build the sanctuary in the inner courts where no one was ever allowed to
enter, not even the Jews. Even Herod had never dared to put
his foot therein. So after years of hard labor a royal house of
marble had been erected to the God of Israel.

The first shafts of morning light began to shine on the
golden pinnacles, the tall bronze gates were beginning to
emerge out of the shadows as if to sing the praises of the Lord
in blaring notes struck by the rising sun. Like every good
Israelite, Zachary was both proud and jealous of the glory of
the Temple, which was the glory of the Ineffable God Him-

self. As there was only one God in Heaven, only one chosen people on earth, so there was only one Temple in the world. Other peoples were idolaters, and therefore looked upon by the Jews as rejected, because their gods were made by hands, the images of demons.

As Zachary gradually approached the Temple, its bulk loomed to gigantic size and seemed to rise up out of porticoes and portals, dominating the surroundings like an immense fortress overlooking the Holy City. Arriving in Jerusalem, Zachary ascended the steps into the Temple where he assisted in some of the ceremonies; then, withdrawing into the priests' quarters, he refreshed himself with a little food. In the evening towards sunset time, he put on his long garment as white as snow and with his companions, also of the class of Abias, received his credentials from the outgoing priests. Then he fulfilled his purifications and ablutions. On the following morning at dawn, promptly and scrupulously, he performed the duties assigned him in turn and by lot. One of these—the greatest he could desire—consisted in offering the sacrifice of incense, a privilege very seldom given.

GABRIEL'S MESSAGE

When his hour came, Zachary entered the sanctuary, trembling with emotion, while the people in the outer court joined the singing of the Levites and other priests, amidst the flare of trumpets. All the people, both within and without Jerusalem, were asking through the mouth of the priest for the assistance of the God of hosts to fight for them unto victory after the hard trials they had endured as a conquered people. With burning invocations the people pleaded for the quick coming of the Messiah, everywhere expected.

It was the fullness of time, and every mother of the line of David hoped to give her nation the King who would avenge its power; and all parents rejoiced to bring children into the world because they hoped they might see the Messiah—the Anointed of the Lord—and might enjoy His reign with joy and gladness.

Trembling, but with a holy pride, poor Zachary felt more than ever the sting of his wife's barrenness because of which their gray hairs were denied the crowning joy of offspring: the joy of a child who would go into battle for the Messiah. According to the rite he placed the live coals on the brazier and poured incense over them. A cloud of perfume arose in soft spirals, spreading over the table on which rested the Loaves of Proposition and floating to the seven-branched golden candlestick; then it ascended slowly like a soft coverlet of perfume floating under the splendid vault, caressing the angels whose outstretched wings graced the veil of the Holy of Holies. Having completed his offering Zachary bowed himself to the ground to pray to the Almighty for his people and for himself. In the heart of this holy man a great fear mingled with the sorrow of a childless father. Once more he asked for the Messiah for his people and a child for himself, associating one with the other as he prayed with sobs.

And behold, in the midst of his prayer an angel appeared at the right side of the altar as suddenly as a streak of light. Zachary had read and had heard many times of angels, but he had never seen their glory so that he was filled with fear and stood as one petrified.

"Fear not, Zachary," said the angel, calling him by name in order to give him courage. "Do not be afraid; thy prayer has been heard, and thy wife Elizabeth is to bear thee a son, to whom thou shall give the name of John. Joy and gladness shall be thine, and many hearts shall rejoice over his birth, for he is to be high in the Lord's favor; he is to drink neither wine nor strong drink; and from the time when he is yet a child in his mother's womb he shall be filled with the Holy

Ghost. He shall bring back many of the sons of Israel to the Lord their God, ushering in his advent in the spirit and power of Elias. He shall unite the hearts of all, the fathers with the children, and teach the disobedient the wisdom that makes men just, preparing for the Lord a people fit to receive him."

Such was the message, sweet and tremendous which only increased the terror of the priest. He understood the meaning very well; a most dramatic meaning—he would have a son destined to prepare his people for the coming of the Messiah; a son with the power of Elias. What an immense honor! Every Israelite knew what the task of the Precursor demanded — he would have to prepare the people for Christ. This honor was falling upon Zachary and his wife Elizabeth, both well bent with age. Could it be possible? The doubt that he might be the victim of an hallucination or the victim of his own vehement desires was a dark shadow crossing all that bright light and he said so. So Zachary replied to the angel, "By what sign am I to be assured of this? I am an old man now, and my wife is far advanced in age?"

Zachary had always trusted God with humble fear; now at this decisive moment he was thinking more of his own old age than of the Eternal One Who is eternal youth. Zachary was wanting in faith. God struck him, thus giving him the first sign by which he would know. And the angel replied, "My name is Gabriel, and my place is in God's presence; I have been sent to speak with thee, and to bring thee this good news. Behold, thou shalt be dumb, and have no power of speech, until the day when this is accomplished; and that, because thou hast not believed my promise, which shall in due time be fulfilled."

And so speaking, the angel like a flash of flame disappeared into the thin cloud of incense. Only the humble old priest was left in confusion, prostrate at the foot of the altar, trembling with an emotion he could not control and a joy he knew not how to define.

Outside the people were waiting. The priest, offering the sacrifice within the sanctuary, was supposed to remain there only a few minutes. He should never linger because the sanctuary is where God dwells, and men should remain outside as much as possible. When the chanting stopped, the faithful waited, then they began to wonder and to whisper, not knowing what to think; until at last the old man appeared in the doorway, bent and trembling.

The people stared at him and their amazement grew beyond measure when he pronounced the formula of blessing although no words issued from his mouth. Only the gesture of his hand imparted the priestly blessing in a silence that chilled all hearts. It was evident to all that something extraordinary had happened: a miracle. The people understood from the signs he made with his hands that there was indeed a divine vision, and they departed in awe. The angel of the Lord had passed over their heads. What was to happen to Israel?

Although deeply moved with emotion, Zachary the priest with his mute tongue continued his duties to the end of the week, thus finishing the course of his office. He felt himself bound more than ever to God in Whose miraculous power he now moved and lived. At the end of the week he started once more on his return journey to the mountains.

His wife Elizabeth was waiting for him with an anxiety which increased with their years. She was standing at the edge of a threshing floor from which one could view a long stretch of the road leading to Jerusalem. When she saw him appear, sitting on his donkey, although a light rain was falling and it was the sunset hour, she felt a sense of relief and thoughts of thanksgiving filled her heart. Quickly she went to meet him. One can easily imagine her emotion when she discovered that her husband could not speak. The mute tongue became the wonder and awe of their kinsfolk and of the entire village.

Maternity now possessed Elizabeth and her heart throbbed with the happiness of youth as she secretly thanked God without ceasing for having liberated her, even in her old age, from the shame of sterility, remembering her as He had Abraham's wife Sarah. For the sake of modesty and because of her years, she hid herself for five months.

In the sixth month, once more the archangel Gabriel came from the presence of God. This time he did not descend directly down into the Temple of gold and marble, but like a shaft of sunlight he soared north, crossing the whole of Palestine seeking a humble village of mud and stones built around a well in Galilee.

The Message to Mary

It was a day like any other day in Palestine; as usual, within the Empire, people were busy feeding their flocks, digging in the soil, talking aimlessly in the streets and trafficking in the marketplaces. Outside the Empire starving tribes fought one another, either for peace or for pastures, as they had always done. Amidst the general indifference of men the most divine event in all history was taking place.

At a sign from God—a sign that had been fixed and decreed from Eternity in the designs of God—a most beautiful archangel, leaving the celestial choir, carrying with him the hope of all the heavenly hosts, darted through space, flashing from star to star towards a tiny planet—the Earth. With a single glance he scanned its crusty surface, patched here and there with stretches of water, and chose a barren country flooded in sunlight—Galilee. There he singled out a miserable little village—Nazareth. It was only a few dwellings huddled together haphazardly on a scorched elevation of ground at the foot of Mount Tabor.

Instead of huddled, we should rather say they were squatted together, for their inhabitants had installed themselves in natural caves, whose entrances were squared off with a bit of plaster, and this entrance served for both chimney and window. The floors were of dried mud partly covered with mats. The inhabitants of Galilee did not enjoy a very good reputation in Palestine, nor did the inhabitants of Nazareth enjoy a good reputation in Galilee itself.

And behold, it was there that the resplendent archangel darted down from heaven like a blade of gold from the sheath of the sun. He was coming from the indescribable bosom of God and looking for the entrance to one of those grottoes used as a dwelling place. Within the grotto he entered, a maiden was praying as she worked. Into the bare walls were inserted some props over which skins were stretched. On the floor were a few working utensils. In this room, the maiden, unknown to the world, was lost in God.

No one perceived the golden furrow made by the angel's flight. Men satisfied themselves with these mud hovels and the pleasures of the flesh and called it "living." As soon as the angel entered, the young girl saw him because she was absorbed in God. She saw him and she was amazed, but not afraid. No doubt, she was accustomed to these appearances.

When the heavenly messenger saw her his eyes shone with tears of joy. The gentle vibrations of his resplendent wings cast a dazzling light over the pitchers of clay, the sheep skins, the working tools scattered about. The crevices of the room, so robed in golden light, stood out like improvised cathedral pillars. The poor room, flooded in liquid splendor, seemed to be an enclosed Paradise.

The divine messenger bowed himself low on the mat and greeted her thus: "Hail, thou who art full of grace! The Lord is with thee; blessed art thou among women!"

The words were few, limitless in their simplicity and

limpid like drops of light; their echo seemed to ascend from the sacred scrolls wherein the Prophets had recorded their predictions, and now they were quoted by an archangel. Spoken in that place, what could be their meaning?

This young girl was the humblest and poorest of all creatures. How could the Lord stoop to her, and how could an archangel believe that she was, indeed, the greatest of all women? She knew of no angelic being who had ever bowed himself down in an act of veneration to any human being. What was happening now? Since she was very young and innocent, she was troubled. She did not understand; and yet, rather, she did understand that the angel had uttered words heavy with mystery, words which were not wholly unfamiliar to her prayerful soul.

"Full of grace"—it meant clothed in all the gifts of heaven.

"The Lord is with thee" indicated a spiritual union between the Most High God and this girl of Nazareth: this was a preparation and a condition for the unity of espousals from which Christ would be born. In fact, "blessed among women" was a sign of the dignity reserved for the Mother of God according to the Sacred Scriptures, poetry of the liturgy and well-known legends.

But how could this be done, since she had consecrated her virginity to God and could never become a mother? In order to be entirely God's she had cut herself off by her vow from carnal union with any man. This humble maiden hidden in a cave in Galilee could hardly believe that God had chosen her for this great dignity; and that having espoused herself to God, God should now espouse her to Himself.

Gabriel saw her tremble like a reed in the sea breeze at dawn. So he explained, "Mary, do not be afraid; thou hast found favor in the sight of God. And behold, thou shall conceive in thy womb, and shall bear a son, and shall call him Jesus. He shall be great, and men will know him for the Son of God the Most High; the Lord God shall give him the throne of his father David, and he shall reign over the house of Jacob eternally; his kingdom shall have no end." These words fell like drops of golden music from the lips of the angel, piercing her whole being with arrows of light that almost dazzled her. The movement of his wings and the bowing of his locks cast lights and shadows over the walls of the room as the marvelous drama unfolded like a divine liturgy.

Mary alone, immersed in the splendor of a mystery which held in suspense God on the one side and humanity on the other, pondered on what it all could mean. How could such greatness be offered the daughter of those who till the soil; and how could a hut made of mud become the palace of a realm? The Son of God was mentioned, and in that name alone the confines of the grotto were pushed back infinitely because heaven and earth were meeting there. It meant this: she, the virgin, who had renounced forever the hope of every Jewish girl to be the mother of the Messiah, was now chosen from among them all for this great act which Israel and the entire humanity after Israel, had been longing for again and again. "How can that be?" she asked after a breathless pause, "since I have not the knowledge of man?"

Gabriel was waiting, with an emotion shared by all the angelic hosts of heaven as well as by all men on earth, the dead and the living and those who were yet to be born—all waiting for her consent. On the consent of that innocent girl depended the Redemption of all mankind. On her depended the rebirth of all the living; from that tender bosom upon which two slender hands were pressed in the attitude of prayer would come the Redeemer.

No, Mary knew not man, nor would she ever know man. She knew only God. She, now in union with God, had not and was not to know any carnal relationship with man. The miraculous was now budding forth—divine maternity within human virginity.

And Gabriel, whose ardent anticipation enkindled his love, seemed to press her as he pleaded, "The Holy Spirit will come upon thee, and the power of the most High will overshadow thee. Thus that holy thing which is born of thee shall be known as the Son of God."

This was as immensely clear as it was immensely mysterious. She was the spouse of the most High: the spouse of the Spirit of God. And from these nuptials between humanity and divinity a Son would be born; from God the Father, and from Mary the mother, was born the Son of God. So she, the adoring creature kneeling on a mat, would be the Mother of God! If grace had not already possessed Mary, she would have collapsed under so immense a revelation; under a responsibility in which heaven seemed to lean on her frail shoulders as though seeking a new center, and earth seemed to cling to her to regain the heights from which humanity had fallen. While Mary in her confusion and astonishment was yielding, the archangel continued to pour his persuasive words like a divine essence into her ears, detailing the immediate circumstances which were both simple and miraculous.

"See, moreover, how it fares with thy cousin Elizabeth; she is old, yet she too has conceived a son; she who was reproached with barrenness is now in her sixth month, to prove that nothing can be impossible with God," he continued.

This evidence was the key. Mary always knew and believed that God could do all things. Behold, He now makes a mother of a sterile woman, and He espouses a virgin to the Holy Ghost. Mary did not will, nor had she ever willed, except what God willed. She had consecrated herself to Him when a child, abandoning herself wholly to Him, so this time also she humbly gave her entire self to Him. And Mary said, "Be-

3. *Nazareth*

hold the handmaid of the Lord; let it be done unto me according to thy word."

It was her consent—simple and explicit—like God's action. It was the consent that opened the drama between heaven and earth; that sealed the collaboration of Mary with God; that gave to Jesus the Mother He had ever desired from eternity. Redemption began at that moment. Carried by the very force of his joy, the archangel seemed to spring in a flash back to heaven to bring the news that held heaven suspended in bliss.

THE SECOND EVE

Mary returned to her solitude and the room was filled with twilight. She was alone; most likely her parents were dead, and though legally she had been entrusted to some relative, in reality she had only God for both mother and father. Her solitude in the world united her more securely to the most High.

Following upon the announcement of the angel, Mary's whole person became invested with the Holy Spirit, and she now became the center of adoration for the angelic hosts. Her poor little dwelling was filled with marvels. In the renewed silence, and vibrant with emotion, the thought must have come to Mary of the destiny of another woman so similar to her own and yet so different: Eve, the mother of all living. All people enlightened by the Gospel should keep this comparison in mind—Mary now represents humanity in God. As soon as the Faithful everywhere study the credentials of their Baptism, their re-birth, they will see with amazement the parallel destinies of the two women—one the mother of fallen humanity, the other the mother of regenerated humanity.

The scene of the archangel at Nazareth corresponds to the scene of Satan in Eden. The atmosphere, however, of Eden was different. Whereas Eden was filled with the enchantments of a fresh nature, exuberant with joy in a dwelling place designed for those unique creatures of such beauty, Adam and Eve; Mary lived in a rustic cave well suited to guard her humility. Eve's virtue was dissipated by luxuriant nature whose glamorous colors could entice her to pride, while Mary's virtue was locked within the walls of a bare grotto, as in a case of rock.

Each one believed the enticing voice of an angel. Eve believed the deceitful flattery which placed her in direct opposition to God and whose commandment she was induced to disobey through her pride; from the depths of her humility Mary believed a commandment which united her entirely to God. In a word, one believed an enemy of God and the other believed an angel from God. There were two assents: one led to death, the other to life. Naïvely, the writers of the Middle Ages remarked that the Ave undid the Eva.

Thus Christ is the new Adam, Head of a regenerated race, and Mary the new Eve, mother of the living who are rescued from eternal death. A virgin introduced death: a virgin has introduced a new life. Oh, Prodigy of Virginity! And its consequences are eternal. From the first virginity was initiated the fall of humanity which unfolded like an uninterrupted landslide bounding from precipice to precipice towards the abyss of eternal death; from the second virginity came the return flight by which humanity ascends cliff by cliff to the throne of God.

"O blessed virgin who hast changed Eve's tears into joy." [2]

And if all humanity was in the bosom of the first mother from whom a long lineage descends, now centuries old, the second Mother brought forth Christ in Whom are all things, and Who is Head of the Church; this second Mother has concurred in destroying the order established by Adam and Eve.

---

2 Petrarch, "Canzome Citata," 35–36.

Therefore was Mary called "the flower of womanhood," "the ornament of her sex." And since her sex was debtor to man (Eve having been taken from the side of Adam), that debt was paid when the new Adam was born without the intervention of man. We have, therefore, a rehabilitation of the flesh and the rehabilitation of womanhood through Mary.

Through a woman we had primarily fallen. Eve had used her womanly grace to drag her companion into sin, and in her the entire sex had received a special condemnation. At the same time the promise was made to Eve that woman would be saved through childbearing. Behold now, womanhood and all humanity with her would be saved through the birth of Jesus from the womb of a Virgin. He Who sums up all humanity in Himself gave to the womb of a Virgin a new and unique dignity.

> The saint of Saints,
> The progenitor of God
> And first of Mothers;
> Virgin and Mother divine;
> First and unique,
> Has glorified the feminine sex.
>   St. John Damascene

In St. Jerome's version of the Bible where he gives the prophecy that refers to Mary, he says that the Lord God *thundered* it from heaven, "I will put enmities between thee and the woman, and thy seed against her seed." In the struggle, however, the woman will be victorious. And if in the Hebrew text the same phrase may seem to refer to Christ, the meaning remains unchanged inasmuch as Mary draws all her value from Christ. Certainly in the divine economy Mary stands opposed to Lucifer, repairing on the part of creatures all the ruin wrought by him which was an abyss of death. And where he had sought to raise himself through pride,

Mary was elevated through humility and she has filled the abyss of death with life.

On this account Mary has often been compared to the virgin soil of Eden which brought forth fruit without seed. As the earth that blossomed in the earthly Paradise, so Jesus flowered forth from her. And finally, if from the corrupt mind of a woman disease came into being, from the intact body of a woman a new spiritual health was attained.

> A woman it was, who opened the door of death;
> A woman, it was who re-called us to life.
>
> SEDULIO

The Fathers of the Church unfold this dualism to the very end: to the tree of perdition, they oppose the tree of salvation—the Cross. Some pious writer has even imagined that the skull of Adam buried at the foot of the Cross, drank the Blood of Christ, the Second Adam while the Second Eve standing close to the cross was sharing in the Passion. Thus between the two principal facts of man's history—the Fall and the Redemption—a bond of blood has been established. Then was begun the life of the Church, of which Mary stands a symbol. In this also Mary was like, and yet different from Eve who was first given as a symbol of the Church when she was formed "as a helpmate to man."

THE ONE WITHOUT STAIN

At the moment of her consent, Mary conceived the Son of God: that is, she brought to pass a mystery inconceivable to mere human thought. By a miracle humanity was inserted into divinity, and divinity into humanity, thereby soldering the two separated by the searing wound of sin. The flesh that received condemnation through Eve, now clothed the Divine Word through Mary: a sign that Mary's flesh was all pure,

pure as flesh had been in Eve before the Fall, pure as when it came from the hands of the Omnipotent Creator. Thus, the very instant the Lord espoused His servant, the action of Reparation began.

And what a Reparation! It was a reintegration which gave us more than was lost since it associated humanity with God Himself. Man, with Eve, had given himself over to Satan; God, with Mary, now gave Himself to man. He was coming to dwell with us in the house of Mary, in her very arms.

The mystery is so complex that it bewilders the mind, and yet so simple that it ravishes the heart; one recognizes the simplicity of God's way. He Who had taken clay to make of it the king of creation, now took a humble maiden to make of her the divine instrument (in the physical order) for the insertion of divinity into humanity. This was necessary for its re-creation, after its fall into death. It was an act of spontaneous humiliation on the part of the Son of God that He might raise men to the new status as sons of God after they had been bastards of Satan.

In this theandric economy, in this second act of creation, Mary was placed at the very center—the point of confluence for the love of the Father and the hopes of us, His children; she is the prodigious link of reunion, thanks to the nuptials celebrated in a paradise transferred and enclosed in the hole of a cave.

Thus something immense has happened—an act of love such as only a God could make—the indwelling of God and His formation into a man within the bosom of a maiden, which bosom became an infinite Paradise. The One to be born of her was to come as a King. Her lap would serve Him as a royal palace; where the King would live and where his treasures would be guarded. Her bosom was worthy of a king and prepared from Eternity to be His dwelling; she was worthy of God and pure beyond humanity's purity.

Mary was the "forma Dei," the seal of God; she was to mould a God-man, give Him her blood and form His limbs. This she did, and in her womb, like all other mothers, she moulded the mind of the child to be born of her. She made Him somewhat a copy of herself; the All-pure could only come from what was all-purity. It was for this purpose that Mary had been conceived in her own mother's womb without Original Sin. The fruit of the Precious Blood of Christ was applied to her by anticipation, that Blood which was also her blood.

All this is most extraordinary, and yet most obvious. We can understand why the archangel called her "full of grace." In Baptism men receive some measure of grace, she had the *fulness* of it. Christ is the whole of Grace, she had Christ in her bosom, He grew in her, she fed Him, and then she brought Him up.

This is not some modern discovery, or an explosion of pent-up love; the ecstatic poetry of the Middle Ages sang again and again that Mary was "the rose of heaven, immune from the thorn of the ancient guilt," "Virgin pure and holy before being born." "Offshoot sprung from the root of Eve the sinner, but immune from the first sin." All this, modern theology has enclosed in a dogmatic definition pronounced by the lips of a Pope.

All is so terse, being divine poetry! From eternity God had foreseen man's fall, and from Eternity the Son of God had offered Himself to repair it: and from Eternity the Spirit of God had chosen a human creature to accomplish the Incarnation through which preparation would be made. The revolt against the Creator began with man, therefore with man reparation must begin. It must be worthy of God and therefore only God could accomplish it. A God-man was needed; and also a mother who would generate the Word made Flesh. Mother of the God-man! What a limitless dignity! It was the very highest possible, and so God chose Mary to perform the tremendous act by which the Infinite inserted Itself into the finite. Could there have been any other instrument for this insertion, or the flowering forth of the Word into Flesh?

No dwelling-place of men was pure enough to be a worthy welcome to His purity; no corner of the earth was beautiful enough to suffer His beauty; no other created element had eminent virtue for realizing the personal ingress of God into the human. There was need of a place which, belonging to man, would possess a purity, a beauty and an excellence proper to God; while being on earth, would be immune from the guilt with which the earth was saturated; where no dark enticings would arise from the flesh, no contacts with sin could ever happen, no shock of passion. There was need of a place of peace equal to that in which the archangels were immersed and which is the very atmosphere of the Trinity; a paradise, circumscribed because of earth, but infinite in value as if it were in Heaven. Thus in the person of One Who is All-pure we are carried back to the beginning of sin and stand facing the one who is *All-Impure*.

The problem of the origin of evil tormented ancient thought quite as much as it does modern thought. It asked itself, "If the world was created by God Who is the Good, it must be as good as the hands that formed it. How then has evil entered into its very vitals?" Evil entered among the most perfect of God's creatures—the angels, precisely because they *were* perfect and had *free wills*. Lucifer and his followers used this liberty to elevate themselves above their proper sphere. Satan was first an Archangel, Lucifer, but he wished to be more. He allowed himself to be caught in pride which is the great anti-social sin of him who refuses to remain in his proper place among his brethren—to love them—but elevates himself above and in opposition to others for his own advantage. Satan passed on to man the abuse of free will, thus enslaving man in sin.

And Satan made use of a woman. It can be truly said—in a sense—that evil entered humanity by becoming incarnate in the heart of a woman, the creature destined to mould and to transmit life by child-bearing. Eve transmitted her own ruined humanity; she begot Satan in her children. But God the Father Who loved men more than He loved Satan and his angels, and because the fault of men had been weakness rather than malice, disposed that as Satan had entered the heart of man through the old Eve, so by a new Eve—another Woman —God would re-enter humanity to wage war on sin. The first Eve, from being mother of the living, now became the mother of the dead. Since the wages of sin are death, Eve stands at the head of a race now centuries old, dwellers in the cities of the dead; while the spirits of the departed were gathering together beyond the grave in darksome expectation as grievous as death.

In Mary, by a decision of Infinite Love, God solved the problem of Reparation by the Sacrifice of His Son: a problem that implied an immense fact surpassing all measure and imagination—the INCARNATION OF GOD. God could certainly become Incarnate, that is, become man. Being Omnipotent He can do all things, all except evil, but to become man in Eve's lineage meant in a sense to contract a bond with a nature stained with sin, and this God would not do.

Then the Father had recourse to the stupendous miracle of this adolescent girl. She stood against Satan the proudest of creatures, as the humblest of creatures, the one most abandoned to the Lord her God, and whom He created untouched by sin. God made her IMMACULATE, with a womb as pure as the dwelling place of God in Heaven, so that God might dwell therein on earth.

In that marvelous privilege humanity began to be re-created, and where it was not already obscured by pride, even unto blindness, it was focused in this creature who brought the Redeemer from heaven to earth.

This woman of such unique exception did not wear costly adornment or ostentatious garments. She was attired as the poorest and simplest of people, because God uses the good and simple things in His work. Her wonderful privilege was not an exterior one, it was in her heart, where in other creatures the seed of sin has its dwelling place. Free will, which Eve had abused, also concurred in this divine miracle, because the rectitude of Mary's will was a positive contribution: she was free in time so that in the epoch of her life there could take place the greatest compact with the love of the Father Who would again gather together His wandering children. The Creator was receiving back the immortal souls dispersed by death; it was a contribution which possessed all the attraction of an Ineffable Tryst.

The reconciliation of the Creator with humanity began in Mary's heart. She was the Divine Mother and the human creature physically bound to Christ, the Son of God, because she was part of humanity. She initiated the great work of reuniting, through which she gave God back to men and men to God. She is Mother of Christ and mother of Christians; Mother of God and mother of men.

The Incarnation

The Word Himself
In the womb of the Virgin dwelt
Like a Divine Seed,
And was by the Virgin conceived
With her pure blood.

St. John Damascene

The Virgin and the Incarnation

Simple and chaste were the elements by which God wrought the Incarnation. The whole Divine Economy is woven in simplicity, God being Simplex: One. So the Word came from Infinity into the finite, from the highest summit of Heaven He descended to the lowest of planets, into the poorest of regions, to the meanest of homes, and among the most despised people. He took for a Mother, a maiden most humble, chosen because she was so humble. The nearest point to the greatest glory is the deepest point of humility. An ascending movement of the human came to meet the descending movement of the Divine: and this was Mary's work invested by the Holy Spirit. God was INCARNATED. Mary, in the measure in which she was filled with the Spirit of God, and as much as was possible for a creature, was *deified*. Chosen by the Father, espoused to the Holy Spirit, Mother of the Word, she was "the banquet hall of the Trinity." This honor was given her because she was most worthy of it, "the blessed among women."

The Word was bringing to lost humanity Redemption and Grace; because it was Mary who brought Christ who gives us both Redemption and Grace. Through her, Divinity descended among men: through her, humanity ascended to God. These were the two operations that met and became one in her womb; she was really Mother of God, and spiritually mother of men.

Thus in an instant, there began in a place that was of time and Eternity, the entire mystery of the Redemption. By taking flesh the Son of God had by that very fact, taken the Cross and generated His Church. Taking flesh from a woman, He embraced the whole of humanity, and as its Head, He was the Regenerator of it, representing it before God. All this was done in her womb at the "fiat" of Mary. This complex act, with such eternal consequences, was accomplished by the Father in Heaven and by Mary on earth; as her will concurred in the act, so her flesh was associated with it. Through the universal sin of the entire race, the whole earth had rotted in impurity and people were no longer the children of God; they were now an aggregation of slaves belonging to Satan. They knew none of God's mercy and they had lost His love. The human race was lost.

Mary would now bring forth a race to whom God would give Divine mercy; a new people of God in whose veins love flowed. She regained the purpose of mankind, putting order into the creation that had sunk into disorder. Mary possessed all the gifts of nature and grace for this measureless task. She was holy, with a holiness translated into beauty. Even if she had not possessed beauty of form, this maiden of Palestine would have radiated the beauty of her unique purity. In her eyes shone a reflection of the Eternal, and in her person appeared the complete beauty of the Creator's work untouched by Satanic contagion. It is sin, the germ of death, that corrodes what God, the perfect Artist, has created.

> As the rose is born from the thorny stem,
> So Mary was born from Judah.

Thus the students of the Quadrivium sang; a rose so beautiful that there had been none like it in all the past, nor would there be another so marvelous in all the future.

The Gospels say nothing about her birth, nor about her parents: we see the rose when it blooms, we do not see it when it germinates.

> It appeared at Vespers,
>   the morning star,
> It was light to darkness
>   and salvation to ruin.

The Apocryphal accounts give us the names of Anna and Joachim as her parents. Christianity has known little and next to nothing about them, and yet they are much loved. They must have been great saints and, therefore, they have remained great patrons, since they gave to Jesus and to men, the Virgin Mary. Pious and God-fearing parents, they consecrated to God and to the service of the Temple in Jerusalem the daughter born to them in their old age. This we know for certain, that Mary was a virgin, as was foretold to the people in the prophecy of Isaias.

Destined as she was to collaborate in the Incarnation, it was obligatory that she be born pure and remain immune from all contact with man. In matrimony two become one flesh and so the Original Sin of one is given to the other. And for this same reason, beyond being a pure virgin she was IMMACULATE from her conception; for no seed of sin could enter the womb created to receive All-Purity Itself.

"I have called her Mary," Anna would have prayed according to the Koran of Mohammed. "To Thee I entrust her and her posterity, that Thou keep her free from Satan." Thus,

even the sacred book of the Mohammedans declared that
Mary was preserved from Satan, and that she was a virgin.
From her infancy she had vowed her virginity to God. However, in the ancient world for a woman to live alone, even in
Judea, was something unknown and unimagined. Woman,
in all classes and in all states of life belonged to some man,
a husband or a father, a son, a brother, a tutor, only a woman
of bad repute lived alone.

Therefore, the parents of Mary, Joachim and Anna, whom
God had favored in guarding the flower transplanted from
Heaven to this black earth, had promised her, or betrothed
her to a young man, Joseph, who though poor was noble and
upright, and who was a descendant of David, the most illus-
trious king of Israel. Although of royal descent, he was a carpenter by trade, like many others of royal descent at that
time. His austere observance of religion, more than his blood,
kept him conscious of his royal dignity. Mary also belonged
to that royal line, so according to custom her parents were
glad to find a husband for her of the same lineage. A spouse
so God-fearing as Joseph would be able to appreciate and
protect the chastity of his bride, living with her as a brother;
like many of the Israelites of strict observance called the Es-
senes, loving as the stars love one another.

Mary was, therefore, betrothed to Joseph; after which,
according to custom, she remained another year in the home
of her parents. Perhaps it was during this period that these
died, leaving her alone with God Whom she served. It was
then that the archangel had come with the message about the
Divine Conception. Since this maiden looked upon herself
as a servant for the hand of the most High, she did not become proud, she sank into adoration at the designs of God
Who was choosing her, the least, for the greatest of works.
From that instant her adoration was concentrated on that
Divine Seed now germinating in her bosom.

As for herself, she remained outwardly the same; devoted to her home duties, and dependent upon her nearest relatives. When she received the message that Elizabeth her cousin was also with child by divine favor, her immediate impulse was to go and assist her. Divine Power was moving over their heads, and as for them, innocent, simple creatures, they continued their ordinary way of living.

Covered with a veil and carrying on her head a basket containing some bread and a few gifts for her relatives, she joined one of the caravans that were going up to Jerusalem for the paschal feasts; probably introduced and recommended by her relatives to some acquaintances in that group. It was a long journey and she started with all the serene fortitude of the innocent trusting in God. She was carrying God in her womb; she was the one, blessed among women; but the consciousness of this dignity did not disturb her tranquil humility even for an instant: like Jesus, she always considered herself at the service of everyone.

The caravan walked during the cool hours of the morning, the evening and part of the night; the Jews kept their liking for a nomad existence. During the starry nights, Mary imagined she could see the wanderings of those mysterious people towards the dawn of a rising sun which they, by their desires for the Messiah, both hastened and delayed. In the night of centuries prophets had arisen like stars to show the way and to point out the direction; to kindle anew their yearning for the Messiah. The fathers and sons of the twelve tribes had walked together straight towards that stream of light; they were poor, torn, down-trodden, falling, but they rose again and went on. From that point of Light, there would spring the miraculous Son of Judah Who would win back Israel's freedom.

How many times Mary had heard the prophecy of the strong Isaias read, according to which, at the end of a period of mourning and misery, the miracle of the virgin-mother would come to pass. "Behold, a virgin shall conceive and bear a son . . ." So, it was she who would be the miraculous flower in whose womb was formed the Redeemer; or, as the Scripture puts it, she was the stem sprung from the root of Jesse, destined to bud forth the Messiah. His Divine Nature would find Its greatest witness in her unspotted virginity, just as His human nature would take on a reality from the reality of her body. In her was wrought the miracle that so amazed the first generations of Christians, the miracle of the union of the two natures in the person of the God-Man.

Walking along through the sleeping country, the call of a shepherd could be heard, the bleating of sheep and the tinkling of a bell, or the sound of the hoof of a she-ass hitting a stone. The other travelers also recalled the prophecies, whose solemn rhythm gave strength to their feet and wings to their hearts. As for Mary, she was hearing the strange words of Jeremiah to the virgins of Israel echoing within the cloister of her heart. ". . . the Lord hath created a new thing upon the earth, A WOMAN SHALL ENCOMPASS A MAN." Jer. 31:22. Words that had seemed veiled were now revealed in all their clear light: she a virgin would give life to a man-child with her own flesh, and hers alone; returning the gift to Adam who in the first creation clothed a woman in his flesh.

The second generation was taking place—the Re-generation. In the secrecy of her bosom she was making this gift to humanity without the contact of man: just as the prophet had spoken of a re-creation of men, and not as of one man alone. In her blood there was budding forth the head of the new Israel, the Head of the Church, therefore the *whole* Church, inseparable from Its Head. A true Eve—that is, Life—she was generating in herself all the redeemed, for they would be the truly living.

She was not exalted by all this; on the contrary, she saw

Figures
of Mary
Most Holy
in the
Old
Testament

RACHEL — *A. Panigati*

Laban had two daughters. The younger, Rachel, was beautiful. Jacob loved Rachel. So Jacob served seven years for Rachel, and they seemed to him but a few days because of his love for her.   GENESIS 29

Rachel's extraordinary beauty was an eloquent image of Mary's ineffable beauty which was the fruit of her great virtues.

RUTH — *A. Panigati*

The field Ruth entered to glean after the harvesters happened to be the section belonging to Booz. . . . Booz took Ruth and married her. Ruth bore a son and they called him Obed. He was the father of Jesse, the father of David. RUTH 2, 4

. . . The Angel Gabriel was sent from God to a virgin betrothed to a man named Joseph, of the house of David and the Virgin's name was Mary. LUKE 1

JUDITH — *A. Panigati*

Judith said: Praise ye the Lord our God who hath not forsaken them that hope in Him. And by me His handmaid He hath fulfilled His mercy which He promised to the house of Israel. And He hath killed the enemy of his people by my hand this night.   JUDITH 13

By becoming the mother of the Word Incarnate, Mary crushed the head of Satan, the enemy of mankind, and freed humanity from slavery.

ESTHER — *A. Panigati*
The king loved Esther and she had favor and kindness before him and
he set the royal crown upon her head and made her queen. ESTHER 2

With the splendor of her virtues Mary won God's love and gave the
world the Word Incarnate.

FAIR AS THE MOON —

A. Panigati

Thou art the glory of Jerusalem, thou art the joy of Israel, thou art the honor of our people. The hand of the Lord hath strengthened thee and therefore thou shalt be blessed forever. JUDITH 15

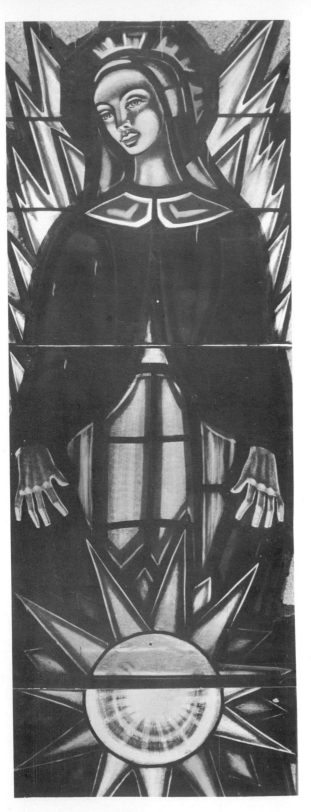

BRIGHT AS THE SUN —
A. Panigati
Listen, O house of David! The
virgin shall be with child, and
bear a son, and shall name him
Emmanuel.   Isaia 7

more clearly—even by physical contact—the greatness of the Divine Creator Who could use an unknown village maiden in an undertaking so excelling the power and intelligence of man.

When within sight of Jerusalem, the caravan began to recite the prayers of their fathers, which were like a chain through whose links was transmitted the heritage of their religion. For her they were an ever old and ever new joy, for others a sense of thanksgiving, for others still a sense of pride. From now on the Messiah would reign. The more humble among the Israelites waited for a kingdom of the spirit; the less humble and the rich expected a military victory with cavalcades of troops to overthrow their enemies and heaps of spoils to divide. Mary was seeing a cross, like a dark shadow, or a grieving prayer, rising from behind the pinnacles of the Temple standing stiff in its gleaming marbles.

THE VISITATION

After a visit to the Temple, the house of her Father and her Spouse, Mary descended from Jersualem and then ascended towards the village where Elizabeth lived with Zachary her husband, a priest. The village was probably Ain-Karim. At the end of a long walk of four or five days, this most pure maiden had reached the threshold of this well-known house. Standing in the doorway as in a frame, her aged cousin, from the darkness of the inner room, turned and saw her and shaded her eyes with her hand, for the sun of Judea was flaming beyond that brown rectangle.

As if she had issued from the sun, and even more beautiful, Mary stepped forward and, with the reverence that a younger woman owes to an elderly one, saluted her. "Peace be with thee, Elizabeth!" The older woman rose to her feet, seized with a sudden trembling. Those words, that face so resplend-

4. Nazareth

ent with purity, which no one could look upon without seeing God, radiating such joy and such grace that in a sudden
the child in Elizabeth's womb leaped within her. The son
that was expected gave signs of life; and gave, by the impulse
of the Divine Spirit, his salute to the woman who was entering the house, and to the Divine Infant that was being formed
in her.

The soul of Elizabeth, a descendant of the Prophets, was
illumined by this fact. The young cousin stood before her
in the light of a miracle. Elizabeth, inspired by the Holy
Ghost Who loosened the prophetical bonds of one in the
priestly class, now gave expression to poetry instinctive to
an Oriental woman educated in a familiarity with the
prophets and, in the name of future generations, she broke
forth into a salutation which still resounds down the ages.

"Blessed art thou among women, and blessed is the fruit
of thy womb." The same blessing as the angel had named!
Her cousin knew! She, too, had been told by a messenger
from heaven. She was herself privileged by an extraordinary
pregnancy, and destined to bring forth a most singular fruit.
The wife of Zachary the priest had by her words acknowledged in the young maiden a dignity incomparably higher
than her own, one most unique among women. Filled with
sweet emotion, the young girl stood still listening to the unusual words that her cousin was saying as she stretched out
her arms to her.

"How have I deserved to be visited by the mother of my
Lord?

"Why, as soon as ever the voice of thy greeting sounded in
my ears, the child in my womb leaped for joy. Blessed art
thou for thy believing; the message that was brought to thee
from the Lord shall have fulfillment.

"Mother of my Lord! Mother of the Messiah! Mother of
God!" This was a priestly soul inspired, who unveiled the

unique mystery of Mary, whose blessedness came from the fact that she had believed. Zachary was there, and mute, because he had doubted the message of the angel in the Temple. Now Elizabeth extols the merit of Mary's faith which is the first contribution to the Redemption. If Jesus is to give His Blood, humanity must have *faith* in His Blood. Mary was, therefore, the first believer, the mother of Faith.

Elizabeth's beautiful salutation, in which she blessed the Child to be born, calling the young maiden "the Mother of my Lord," thus associating her with the joy of her own imminent maternity, made Mary's emotion overflow. The blood of David flowing in her veins was also rich in poetry, and her relationship to Elizabeth marked her ties to the same sacerdotal family. Standing before her holy cousin Elizabeth who was also the object of a miracle that involved her in the Divine Plan, Mary burst forth in the morning canticle of the Magnificat. It was a joyful outburst of Grace at the very dawn of the Redemption.

"My soul magnifies the Lord." Not herself ever; always the Lord. The miracle and the love was for Him alone. As she praised the greatness of God, Mary, His handmaid, saw her own lowliness elevated to the Divine heights of the Almighty, and she told of the reversal of things her Lord was about to accomplish through her. She saw down the vistas of time, down the coming centuries, millions of human creatures turning to her, singing her praises and calling her blessed. As if through a mist, she saw a forest of Church spires and caught the indistinct murmuring of myriad supplications. She felt herself a mother to all in that endless succession of souls invoking her through the centuries.

MARY, MARY! That name would become the most diffused and the sweetest of all names, thanks to her; it would be filled with a charm never worn out by repetition, and its rendition in every language would never mar it. And in fact, she, the sweetest of all creatures imbued it with such beauty that to any woman, no matter how unfortunate she might be, or how degraded, that name would give some dignity and beauty. There is some thing of regal splendor and lily whiteness in it like the lustre of a pearl. When called by that name, a woman becomes lovely, and by a reflected beauty from the name, she becomes, in a sense, somewhat sacred.

All this was conferred on Mary through the merits of her own humility. Thus God began to build on her humility the ruin brought about by the pride of angels and of men. Her blessedness would return in blessings on all the redeemed who were faithful to God and associated with her. From the very instant of her consent, a Christian revolution was initiated in which the supernatural order would act on the natural order. Thus God, baffling human judgments, entrusted the message of the greatest religious, moral and social revolution ever known to a young girl, well known by those of her times. She was loved for her gentleness and kindness so frequently revealed by a smile; her countenance was never clouded by resentment nor troubled by deceit, and all this happened in a poor village, in the home of two elderly persons, one of whom could not speak.

This revolution, coming from the divine plan, would take hold of the human order. Mary, herself poor but contented with her state, possessing those most valuable riches of faith and love of God (precisely because of her faith and love the sense of justice springing from the fountains of grace so abundant in her, and from her, her meditations on the Scriptures, and coming directly from the Divine Light radiating from her womb) felt and pronounced at once, in the presence of Zachary, the priest, the condemnation of the wickedness under whose oppression the poor groaned.

These injustices were so many that the word *rich*, in a religious sense had become synonymous with the word *iniquity;*

while the word *poor* had come to be synonymous with the word piety, inasmuch as *goodness*, in a materialistic society, brought about only misery. Nevertheless, the great things God had wrought in her, were a proof that God had, in His judgment, already reversed the order sin had established, which is rebellion towards God, by dispersing the proud and pulling down the mighty from their seats, to put the poor in their places. He was sending away the rich and putting the hungry in their stead. And as usual, this overthrow was not so much partial and material, as it was absolute; for the Lord did not stop at overturning economic fortunes. He banished from His heart the rich and the mighty who had withdrawn themselves from the unity preached by the Law, because they trusted in their money and places of power as in things they could never lose, and thus He condemned them to eternal misery. The Mighty One was tearing them down from the heights of their proud thoughts, pulling them out of their imaginary social positions, casting them into the abyss which was a punishment filled with insatiable hunger and infinite subjection. The action of grace did not spare those hard and earthly institutions behind which the materially satisfied take refuge, believing themselves so definitely sheltered and secure. The Lord grasped their privileges and scattered them to the winds.

All this was said in forceful accents, an outburst of prayer enlivened by a touch of the poetical by the blessed one so full of grace, who appeared to the eyes to be a mere girl, perhaps not more than fourteen, but who gave us the first instruction in the Gospel: she, who was the Virgin Mother of Christ Himself, Who is the Gospel. No mouth so gentle will ever again speak such powerful words. She had always been so secluded in her little home, loving her solitude as a protection for the depths of mystical love that enshrouded her. One might have thought her unconscious of the lowly vicissitudes

of earth; on the contrary, because she loved her Heavenly
Father, she loved all people as brothers.

Mary, the young Mother of the Church, not only remembered those humble creatures, God's children who, like herself, toiled day and night to draw a little bread from the
barren soil, but she also carried in her bosom all sufferers, all
the despised of the world, the defeated ones of all the ages
and, separating them in her mind from their servitude, she
judged them as God would, and saw them as they would be in
their immortal dignity and glory. To violate the dignity of
the human person is to violate the rights of God the Creator:
and Mary, the Mother, spouse and daughter of the Trinity,
pronounced the condemnation of those who do so, with the
authority that was hers by her unique privilege.

Most formidable is this gentle maiden, in her canticle and
in her judgment, which, on a level with the Divine Economy
of justice and love, she stigmatizes in accents surpassing the
fury of the Prophets, condemning a human economy made
up of egotism. She does not discuss, she cuts off. Her eyes are
aflame with indignation and with joy. She is sweet, but she is
not soft. She loves, and she is strong for the same reason. She
is the handmaid of God, therefore she is not the slave of false
gods, of the purse, and of vain glory. Since she is deeply religious, she reveals that she is entirely just, terrible as an
army in battle array; with the terribleness of Mother and
Virgin.

And these are the words of her song:

"My soul magnifies the Lord; my spirit has found joy in
God, my Saviour, because he has looked graciously upon the
lowliness of his handmaid. Behold, from this day forward all
generations will count me blessed; because he who is mighty,
he whose name is holy, has wrought for me his wonders. He
has mercy upon those who fear him, from generation to generation; He has done valiantly with the strength of his arm,

driving the proud astray in the conceit of their hearts; he has put down the mighty from their seat, and exalted the lowly; he has filled the hungry with good things, and sent the rich away empty-handed. He has protected his servant Israel, keeping his merciful design in remembrance, according to the promise which he made to our forefathers, Abraham and his posterity for evermore."

This is the song in which the past and the future are joined: the spiritual with the temporal, and all the fathers of Israel meet again, and the children of paganism with them.

As she heard all this, Elizabeth, listening in the name of all creatures who were looked down upon, scorned, and starved by the owners of physical force and of gold, stood enchanted with her face strained and wet with tears. She was vaguely conscious that she was living one of the most solemn moments in the world's history; and in that room where, once the eyes had become accustomed to the dim light, could be seen a shuttle, a few jugs, some tools, a kitten asleep on a mat, and a hen clucking to her chickens.

After having praised the Lord, the young maiden made herself at home in that modest dwelling; the handmaid of the Lord became the handmaid of Elizabeth, the old woman, now pregnant and who had need of her help, so God's mother, with her smiling simplicity, attended for three months to turning the stone that ground the meal in the early morning, caring for the animals and baking the bread.

MARY'S ESPOUSALS

Summer came; and since it was not proper for the virgin to assist at Elizabeth's deliverance, and since her help was needed in Nazareth for the work in the fields, Mary took leave of her cousin, about to give birth to John, the Precursor of Jesus and, in the company of some relative, she started

again on her long journey to Nazareth. The charm that de-
lighted God, though unseen by men, was her calm poise; it
was made up of simple humility, even after the revelations
she had heard of her unique majesty as Mother of the Lord.

Back again among her own people, she resumed her ordinary life of prayer and work, in obedience to her relatives.
Sometimes Joseph would come for a visit. He would talk to
her of his simple projects for beginning their housekeeping
and, with a look of intense veneration, he told her how much
he loved her. All his life was being bound, day by day, like
a climbing plant in bloom, around her purity, who was like
a stock planted in Eden. The poetry of his youth, under the
inspiration of the Scriptural canticles, so well-known to the
fervor of this descendant of **David** the Psalmist, he was moved
to sing them to her in his restrained and sweet voice.

Then behold, one day he perceived in Mary the signs of
pregnancy. A black cloud seemed to settle down on this sincere soul, and he rose to go, terribly agitated. Working alone
in his little house, that thought so occupied his mind that he
could see nothing else. His worry was a torment to him and
he knew not what to think. It seemed to him that all he had
most loved was now taken from him by some inexplicable
evil.

Mary's virtue was well known to him; he knew the integrity of her family; but he had seen the signs of her maternity.
So, confounded, he went about for many days under the torture of the discovery he had made. By the laws of the country,
he had the right to denounce the infidelity of this maiden
betrothed to him, have her brought to trial and probably
condemned to death for adultery.

But Joseph was just; he loved Mary—he loved her in God
—and could never tolerate such a procedure as to expose her
to infamy. His strong moral sense, made delicate by his religion, detected a mystery; and not wishing to cause a scan-

dal, he planned to free her from the bond of their betrothal and secretly leave her. His heart was broken; his dream of being a husband ruined; but he preferred to writhe in the agony of separation rather than to do harm to her whom he loved. It was love—love purified by the law of religion—that saved him from jealousy which could have brought about a catastrophe. He who abides in Love, is in the truth and above justice.

Behold, when he was most tortured by agony and uncertainty, there came to him one night a heavenly messenger, perhaps the same Archangel Gabriel who, up to now, was like a shuttle going from one end of Palestine to the other, weaving the great announcements of the Redemption. "Joseph, son of David," he said to him in a dream, calling him by his title of honor, "do not be afraid to take thy wife Mary to thyself, for it is by the power of the Holy Ghost that she has conceived this child; and she will bear a son, whom thou shalt call Jesus, for he is to save his people from their sins." (Matt. 1:20,21.)

And as a crowning sign, the Archangel recalled the prophecy of Isaias, concerning the virgin destined to conceive the Emmanuel. "And all this was so ordained to fulfil the word which the Lord spoke by his prophet: Behold the virgin shall be with child, and shall bear a son, and they shall call him Emmanuel, which means God with us." Into those words, about the greatest mystery in the religion by which he lived, there now flashed a light on his mass of doubts and obscure understanding. Mary was the spouse of the Holy Ghost, mother of a son who would break the bonds of sin; a liberation that God alone could accomplish. Emmanuel meant "God with us." In anger God had turned away from men: He was returning to men by the virginal way of that maiden, Joseph's betrothed.

At the message, Joseph hesitated no longer; trembling with

gratitude, he embraced the mission entrusted to him, to be the companion and protector of Mary; to fulfill in the eyes of the Law the task of the Holy Spirit Himself, the Heavenly Spouse; and substituting in daily events for the most High, the Heavenly Father, towards the Child Who was bringing the salvation foretold by the Prophets.

Joseph also believed the angel. Like Mary, he had faith, because love for God is shown by faith in His word. In the heart of the carpenter of royal descent, love for the most High in heaven, and for the most pure woman on earth were blended into one worship. Therefore, when the year of betrothal was completed, Joseph espoused Mary. The families of both one and the other gave a feast. The usual nuptial banquet of the poor was celebrated with some lambs or kids, with cakes and fruit and wine; and the happiness of the two who now guarded an incomparable secret, was concentrated on Him Who was to come. A narrow room instead of Paradise served for the workshop and sheltered the physical formation of God.

Joseph was an intelligent young man, whose soul was formed in the spirit of the Scriptures; he was upright, steady and unwavering, always turned in the direction of the Eternal, hence his heart transformed his workshop into a temple where, loving and strong, he watched with anxious care the one whom he loved. He knew now who she was. He had been drawn to her since his boyhood with a sweet reverence, and he knew Who was to be born of her. Joseph stood in need of a courage superior to any eventual slander or malignity, and he possessed it. He also needed a sense of humility, so as not to be over-anxious; and, knowing that the entire miracle was from God, he bowed in humble adoration. Mary had a worthy companion in him. He had the unique dignity of being Mary's spouse; as such he stands in history, as such he triumphs in Eternity.

That Child, according to the prophecies, was not to be born in Galilee but in Judea, and particularly in Bethlehem, the "House of Bread" about five days walk distant from Nazareth. God, Who often adjusts His great designs to our small human events, now made use, as He often does, of political disturbances, to bring this about.

In the City

of David

JESUS—"MARY'S FLOWER"

O blessed and sweet Mary,
Thou hast given us the flower, sweet Jesus.
ST. CATHERINE OF SIENA

Caesar Augustus, now in the fifty-eighth year of his age, having worked hard, began like all wise politicians to think about
his successor. He had formed the Empire, brought about
peace, developed agriculture, increased the birth-rate, pro-
moted commerce, opened new roads and built cities; now, to
pass on his government in good order, he thought of taking
an inventory, to see how many provinces, how many legions,
how many ships and how many allies he had.

The counting was not easy in such a vast stretch of territory but it was done. Then he wished to take a general census
of the people, which would be used for the triumphal in-
scriptions and for the poll-tax, both useful and pleasant. In
every country for these customs in administration, Rome,
whose policy was a broad-minded one, followed the local
usages; and in Palestine where Roman authority kept a tributary king and there were traditional institutions, the custom
was to make such computations by tribes and by families in
their original locality—where the registers of genealogies
and of classes were kept. The tribe of Judah had its center
in Bethlehem, the little town of David, where the Messiah

was to be born according to the prophecy of Micheas seven hundred years ago.

When the proclamation became known Joseph and Mary started for Bethlehem, their city. Winter, with its cold nights, was coming; and Mary's condition had to be regarded, privileged as she was to form Jesus with her own blood for nine months. Later, after her example, the Church, who is a copy of Mary, and like her a Virgin Mother, was commissioned to form Jesus in souls, and the Church will accomplish this formation by her Martyr's blood and her missioners' journeys through the dark nights of the world.

The road our two poor working ones followed was through Samaria. Although it was the shortest of the three that joined Galilee with Judea, it was also beyond measure the hardest. Each had gone alone over it when ascending to Jerusalem. Now, they walked it together; this fact gave a motherly and sisterly sweetness to Joseph's anxiety as he kept observing that serene face, the love of all generations, fearing lest she suffer too much in her condition. He multiplied his attentions, so happy to be of service to her. He would bring her a bowl of hot milk, then a bit of dry fruit, or a wild flower which had escaped the frost; and if a sprinkling of rain made the donkey halt, sniffing the drizzle, Joseph anxiously sought the shelter of a cave, or a tree, or perhaps some hut. Mary thanked him with a smile that came with difficulty because of her physical fatigue. She pulled her mantle tighter about her chest as though to hide the beating of her heart. The Mother of the Lord of the world was sitting on a bow-legged donkey, sheltered for the night in a sheep-fold amidst the howling of sheep-dogs.

When evening came, they stopped in a village. The poor were always ready to help the poor and to supply what was lacking, so a lodging was always offered; as a rule it would be in the stable among the domestic animals. The King of the world was sleeping in a royal seat, in the womb of a Virgin; a lily within a rose, and the Virgin—the Rose—lay down to rest on the mantle Joseph spread for her on some straw (amidst the thorns—her privations) and she was happy because she was the mother of such a King. Here was a royalty so great, it needed no pomp; so essential, that it sought out shacks in which to rest, so that no man could be dazzled by splendor, nor yet ashamed of his home.

Mary and Joseph ate some bread and drank a little water softened with a bit of vinegar, if offered them; and weary with fatigue they went to sleep near their own donkey and the animals of their hosts. The outlines of the shack seemed to fade in the darkness, while within and without, for those who could see with the eyes of the soul, myriad lights trembled like stars among which the angels, adoring, whirled in and out. Now and then the howling of the dogs awoke the very young woman, who, finding herself in such dense darkness and hearing only the breathing of the cattle feared for the child within her. Being the Mother of God did not spare her from fear of men; on the contrary, the consciousness of her unique responsibility only made her sensibilities sharper, but she did not complain. She was doing the Will of her Father; and love for Him Who was to come turned all her pain into joy. Moreover Mary knew that God is served by suffering.

In this way she shared in the mystery of the Redemption which was to be the mystery of sacrifice. Already she was offering to this great Act her anguish, which she offered for Jesus, and His purpose became her contribution towards the Redemption.

The two travelers made one of their first stops at Jacob's well in the neighborhood of Sichem where the memory of the Patriarchs and the expectation of coming events filled them with mystical emotion as they paused under the light of the stars. Farther on they passed by the foot of Mt. Garizim, then continued on in a straight line to Bethel and Emmaus; from Emmaus they ascended to Jerusalem from whence they pushed on in a last stretch to Bethlehem.

Mary, with a sisterly sense of being one with her people, remembered the gentle and sincere Ruth who had followed the reapers on these terraces, gleaning. Booz the master of the harvest admired her thrift and desired her for his wife; from their descendant came King David and fourteen generations later came Mary and Joseph. On these very slopes the young shepherd, their future king had wandered, leading his sheep and dreaming, strong and daring in driving away the wolves. But at this very moment the tragic King Herod of Judea, a murderer of his own sons, was on his way to the Herodium. At the mere mention of his name, Mary shuddered.

THE BIRTH OF JESUS

On the narrow ascending road they passed other travelers going to Bethlehem for the census. Some were disgruntled because their business was interrupted and unattended at home; some cursed this counting of the free sons of the most High as an outrage coming from those who were slaves to idols; others were patient and resigned, seeing in it a punishment of God for the sins of Israel.

The wise ones recognized a divine design in this unforeseen gathering of the descendants of David in the place of their origin and were agreeing with Joseph who suggested that they see in the poor administrative schemes of men the greatest mystery of Divine Providence. In the evening when they finally arrived in the public square of the town, they saw it lighted with lanterns, especially at the entrance to the caravan enclosure. Joseph, like the others, wedged his way through the crowd of noisy travelers and, at the door where men and animals were passing in and out, asked for a place to sleep. The woman with him was in delicate condition and she needed a couch apart from the rest. The bearded innkeeper looked Joseph over from head to foot and seeing his cloak splashed with mud shook his head and replied, "There is no room for thee in the inn." A place might have been found in a large ample inn, but not for a meanly clad carpenter and a Galilean woman about to be delivered of a child.

Joseph knocked at the door of a few private houses but everywhere those who had come for the enrolling had already crowded in; for him, who was of David's lineage, and Mary, the Mother of the Messiah, in the city of David, the native city of the Anointed, there was not so much as the lair of a beast in which to rest. So it would always be for Jesus, the wild beasts would have their holes but He would not find a stone on which to rest His head. Already, before ever He was born, He was beginning His renunciation.

Joseph was not discouraged. On the way up to Bethlehem he had observed some caves in the side of the hill with open entrances and he knew by experience how to lodge in them. Although he was grieved at having nothing better to offer the woman to whom the Archangel had paid such homage, they retraced their steps part of the way and, turning a little outside the village, they reached the entrance of a cave where the cattle were heard peacefully chewing their cuds. Here they entered. Joseph lighted the lantern he had carried and prepared a pallet of hay for Mary, who could hardly walk by this time.

The wind was blowing into the entrance and Joseph sought to ward it off by stretching some mats he had found in the place across the doorway. He covered Mary with his cloak and in the painful silence he prayed to God for her. Thus rested among the slumbering animals the one whom all generations would call "blessed" and to whom the Church in wonderment would apply such titles as "salvation of the world";

"gate of heaven"; "dispenser of all graces"; "the honor of creation"; "abode of the Trinity."

In poetry she would be invoked as the "lamp of the centuries"; and behold, the wick of their lantern was lowering and flickering as if about to die out, while in its tiny light the obscurity of the cave became more dense. At intervals the donkey pawed the floor and the wind carried to their ears the sound of bleating sheep. Joseph was falling asleep and yet he would not sleep, and from time to time he spoke to Mary. She was absorbed in a silence full of the Divine. An interior colloquy was going on between herself the Mother, and God the Father. And the vigorous Peter Damien imagined, in his emotion, that she talked with the unborn Child.

> Who is this knocking at the door
> And breaking my sleep of the night
> to call me?

> O Virgin most fair, my sister, my spouse,
> O gem most splendid hasten to rise,
> Open to me, my sweet one!

Yes, open to me the Life among men, my Evangelization, my Cross. And she opened. Jesus entered the world amidst the darkness, the wind, the solitude and the cattle. The Creator of the sun entered this planet through a cave like the least of those born of woman so that no one could complain of having a meaner condition in life. He also entered as the first-born of woman because He was welcomed by the purest love of a mother. The Father withheld from Him all the splendors of Divine sonship so that He could enclose Himself entirely within the tenderness of human maternity. In that first instant He had no songs of the angels, nor did He come with rumbling thunder; He had the incomparable caress of Mary, beloved daughter of the Father and most lovable little Mother of the Son.

5. *Nazareth*

Under the light of a lantern, she lovingly pressed Him to herself in a transport of joy and wrapped Him in His poor clothes,—her own. Perhaps she used one of her garments or her apron, and her love. After she had covered him against the cold as best she could, and after Joseph had revived the smoky lantern, she raised the little creature against the light to contemplate his face. In it she saw her own features, and the lineaments of her Heavenly Father; then she gave Him her first kiss. In that kiss, she experienced the greatest joy that a mother has ever felt. Her soul shared in the delights of Divine Love and ascended for a second into the heavenly beatitude; a rapture which every common mother feels when kissing her first child for the first time, was in Mary sublimated by adoration; for her lips touched the Eternal God, and in His creature she contemplated her Creator.

Then the low cave was filled with exulting angels and Joseph, weeping for joy, received the Child from Mary's pure hands, and after kissing Him laid Him on the straw in the manger where no breath of wind could reach Him, and where the warmth from the cattle was wafted towards Him. In that royal crib the New-Born took His first sleep.

However great the voluntary humiliations of the King of the universe may be on earth, the rejoicing was great in heaven because the tremendous miracle of Infinite Love had taken place. An angel—perhaps Gabriel once more—flew up from the midst of the peaceful, dreaming cows and betook himself to a flock of sheep, among the shepherds who, wrapped in sheepskins, watched their flocks at the edge of the wilderness. And out of the monotonous darkness they were suddenly surrounded with such a dazzling light that they were frightened.

"Do not be afraid!" said the angel whose silhouette could be seen now and then in a light bright as the sun. "Behold, the news I bring you is good news of a great rejoicing for the whole people."

The shepherds bounded to their feet, looking and listening intently. Then God *was* remembering His people who had seemed abandoned and left to the mercy of the Idumeans and pagans, and was now sending a messenger to *them*, the roughest and most despised class in Judea, repudiated by the scribes of the Law. "This day, in the city of David, a Saviour has been born to you, no other than the Lord Christ. This is the sign by which you are to know Him; you will find a child still in swaddling-clothes, lying in a manger."

So he said, and around the fiery herald swarmed myriad ranks of other angels, radiant divisions of the heavenly army, for that night heaven was emptying itself on earth in a luminous ring of light which followed its Prince, now a dweller upon earth. From their lips eloquent with love, a song burst forth that made the stars quiver with joy: "Glory to God in high heaven, and peace on earth to men who are God's friends."

After that the luminous ranks of angels and their song gradually vanished into the darkness of the night which closed down like a black curtain on the last disappearing one. Those leaders of flocks whose hard life was spent in the fields beneath the open sky, in a monotonous succession of seasons, known by the regular passing of the starry flocks in the black vault above their heads; now, because of their simplicity, had suddenly assisted at the most stupendous spectacle—like nothing else that had ever been recorded in the Sacred Scrolls—and they had listened to the sweetest of messages.

"Glory to God!" This comforted them. It meant that they were like sons, although other men had often acted towards them like wolves. "Peace on earth" consoled them with a spirit of goodwill because in their march to the green hills they had often been drenched in blood by those who sought to conquer and to loot them.

Now they scattered, running over the terraces to Bethlehem, and they were not slow in finding the grotto of the miracle. There they found the Expected One in the form of a frail Infant wrapped in poor bands near its mother, a Galilean girl, perhaps fifteen years old, whose countenance seemed even younger by her pallor and look of love. Since the shepherds were poor and lowly, they were not surprised at her lowliness, and in their simplicity they adored the Son of God. Oh, how the Mother did rejoice at the homage of those simple souls!

Women, who had come with the shepherds, now returned to the sheep fold to fetch milk, cheese, skins of sheep wool, and they vied with one another in offering all to Joseph with the noble generosity of the poor. The women offered that delicate and sisterly help which women know how to give with heroic generosity under such circumstances, although Mary had no need of it, her delivery having been no more than a sweet giving devoid of suffering.

Then in turn, they all came silently, with tears in their eyes to contemplate the face of a Child (they who had lived in breathless anticipation of the Messiah) Who signified the beginning and the end of eternal values: glory, liberty, and above all, peace.

These were shepherds who, in the purest spirit of the Prophecies, understood what such a birth meant in the life of men. They adored God and venerated the Woman, who in generating Christ had generated the salvation of the whole world; and they felt themselves in infinite debt towards such a Mother, who being filled with Grace, was bringing forth Christ—the WHOLE OF GRACE, and gave to those condemned to death through Original Sin the sign of Eternal Life.

The Flower of Mary is Christ. "She is Mary of Nazareth,"

murmured the women, embracing each other in their joy. And leaving the grotto, they spread the word, saying with emotion to everyone, "I saw Him! With my own eyes!" And they added, not knowing how to describe the joy they had experienced, "And I saw His Mother!"

For centuries hosts of believers have envied those on earth who saw with their own eyes Jesus and His Mother and the vigilant foster father Joseph there in the shelter of domestic animals. In the following days other people came; sincere ones, and an anonymous crowd of those whose souls were not entirely hardened by gold; and near the manger, perhaps later in some hospitable little home, Mary would come to meet them, offering them her Son, Who was the Son of God, to look upon. Her Child was like a flower blooming on the stem which was herself, the offshoot of Jesse; and by a gesture of her chaste hands she was already offering Him in a sense, to all people, for all people, conscious of the need of a still greater offering.

MOTHER OF THE LIVING

It is enough simply to recall the Birth and all earth rejoices. Christmas is the children's feast, since childhood innocence is closest to the angels, and the feast of all people whose intellect has not grown old with vice.

> Happy the day,
> Greatest of all days
> Which saw the glory of this birth!
>
> Happy the Mother,
> Who had God for her Child.

Thus sung Abelard in the twelfth century: gathering up the emotions of all past centuries and of all future ones. One

Christmas night during Mass St. Gertrude heard in the singing of the Gloria, the words "Primogenitus Mariae Virginis Matris" (Firstborn of the Virgin Mary, Mother:) she thought that it would be more exact to say "Unigenitus Mariae Virginis" (Only Son of the Virgin Mary), when the Holy Virgin, herself, appeared to her and said with great graciousness, "Do not say that this sweet and lovable Child is my only One: call Him rather my Firstborn: because after I brought Him forth, I have begotten after Him, all of you; or rather, through Him I have made of you all His brothers, thus making you my only begotten sons whom I adopted in the womb of my motherly love where I bear you."

And another nun of the Middle Ages, Rovita, in her ethereal verses, spoke her gratitude in these words:

> Unique. hope of the world, illustrious Lady of Heaven,
> Holy Mother of the King; shining star of the sea;
> You, bringing forth, O Pious Virgin, have made whole
>   for the world,
> The life that the old virgin (Eve) had lost.

Jesus and Mary! The Christian conscience is like a river that carries the riches of Christ's doctrines and knows not how to separate these two names. The Ethiopians always represented the Virgin with the Child. For them, Mary could never be without her Son; nor would the Son be without His Mother. Mussulmen themselves, according to their Koran, never mention Jesus other than "son of Mary," not being able to separate the two.

Christian people turn to the Motherhood of Mary in two great natal hours: their birth to earthly life, and their birth to eternal life, death. Mothers especially turn to her in that mysterious hour when a new life is detaching itself from them; and all entrust themselves to her in a special manner at the hour of death. With her protection they do not fear to cross the great threshold that separates the Eternal from the transitory present, and they present themselves less frightened and unprovided for, before the Judge.

A legend gives the charming story of some sinners whom Jesus had not admitted to Paradise, and He gave orders to St. Peter, the guardian of the gate, not to admit them. Behold, a little later, Jesus saw them walking amidst the flower beds in the heavenly gardens. He questioned the guardian of the gate who answered, "The door is shut, but your mother Mary has opened the window and let them in."

Mary is both the window and the gate of Paradise; for if by her the Word is born to us, we are born to the Word by Mary. And since the work of each Christian is to form Christ in himself, every one of the faithful is mystically imitating Mary when Christ is generated in himself and in others. This is made possible by the fact that He was born of Mary and through Baptism Christ gave us the power to become the adopted children of God, and therefore children of Mary.

"Blessed are the faithful," says St. Ambrose, "because they also have heard and believed, and are become mothers of Christ. Every soul who believes conceives and generates the Word of God." Therefore we are generators of Christ, and associated in Mary's lot; even unto this had God taken hold of us and reunited us to Himself. All this has been possible, thanks to the Maiden of Galilee.

"With the coming of the Son of God, I—a man—have received divinity: I—a mortal—have received immortality; putting aside corruption, I have put on incorruption and received the garment of Deification." A great reversal was initiated that night in the cave, where:

> From a star, the sun was born;
> From a girl, the Son of God
> Came from the sacred fount of her womb.

Daughter of the Son and Mother of the Father;
She is a virgin and yet bears the name of **mother**;
She is virgin, and yet both mother and **daughter**.

Mary

and the Child

The Presentation to the Father

On the eighth day, according to the law of Moses, the new-born Child was circumcised. Since He was the Son of God, He could have dispensed with this bloody rite; having become Man of the Jewish race, He willed to submit to their laws, having taken upon Himself all the burdens of humanity, except Sin, which is inhumanity. In that rite He gave the first tribute of blood, the beginning of that infiltration of a dry earth with the Blood of regeneration.

Mary's countenance paled and then flushed with pain and joy; Joseph gave him the name Jesus already suggested by the angel. From that day it was pronounced among men, the name most venerated and the most hated: the name for which martyrs would die and for which persecutors would kill them; the name whose power overcomes hell; the name whose very composition in Greek signifies teaching and the fruit of Redemption; the name that recalled to the Jews and to the Greeks, the salvation that was Incarnate in Mary's Son.

After the fortieth day, always according to the law, the little family went to Jerusalem for the Purification of the mother, who it was believed had contracted impurity through child-birth; and Mary presented the Child in the Temple. She fulfilled the sacrificial requirements by offering two doves. Wealthy women offered a turtle-dove and a lamb: poor women offered the two doves.

After this Jesus was offered to the Lord by the hands of the Priest. The first act of the Mass was initiated; and the Sacrifice was begun in a remote way. The presentation was a ceremony in which all the first born were acknowledged as belonging to God. Once other Semites immolated this with terrible sacrifices to the god Baal: the Law of Moses substituted for this by requiring the sum of five sicles which signified "redeeming" or "buying back." For Jesus, the rite practiced in those brutal forms by the early Semites would be revived in all its horror on the Cross, then all those born of women would receive Redemption from Him.

While the offering was taking place an old man drew near whose name was Simeon. He was filled with a deep religious spirit, wholly united to God Who revealed to him that he should not die until he had looked upon the face of the Messiah. In expectation of this hope he dragged himself on his tired feet to the Temple, waiting for the mothers who came to present their little ones, hoping to recognize by some sign the one Mother he expected.

That morning the Holy Spirit of God had urged him to climb those steep and narrow streets that ended in the esplanade of the Temple, which rose like a fortress of metal and marble crowning the city. Meeting Mary and Joseph in their happiness and seeing the Infant, his soul was suddenly ravished with joy. He understood at once the meaning of this interior illumination and stopped to gaze with childish delight at the new-born babe. Trembling with emotion he asked the Mother, radiant under her veil, the favor of holding the ruler of the world for a few moments. Mary, who always gives to all who ask, and still gives, held out her babe to him to be seen and embraced as she had offered Him a short time before to her Heavenly Father. The old man, so venerable in his snow-white beard, with a veil of tears in his tired eyes, also raised the Infant-Victim of the unique sacrifice to the Lord, and happy in having reached the goal of his long waiting, exclaimed: "Ruler of all, now dost thou let thy servant go in peace, according to thy word; for my own eyes have seen that saving power of thine which thou hast prepared in the sight of all nations. This is the light which gave revelation to the Gentiles, this is the glory of thy people Israel."

THE SIGN OF CONTRADICTION

A canticle! Joseph listened with amazement, and the Virgin too, with shining eyes. Everywhere her Child brought the signs of a universal rebirth. The good old man spoke words of benediction to them and, returning the precious treasure to His mother, he pronounced a prediction which brought her face to face with her destiny as the mother of One Who would be sacrificed, and associated with Him in His tremendous immolation.

"This Child," he said, "is destined to bring about the fall of many and the rise of many in Israel; to be a sign which men will refuse to recognize; and so the thoughts of many hearts shall be made manifest; as for thy own soul, it shall have a sword to pierce it."

Mary could see behind those innocent limbs the red reflections of flashing swords and ruins and contradictions. She gave love and received a sword. Her Child was coming to offer Himself for the salvation of all men, and men would find in Him a cause for dissension, they would fight and wrangle over His frail Flesh. He brought peace to men of goodwill, and therefore, the anger of men of bad will would be let loose upon Him. Perhaps the poor little mother pressed her Babe to her breast with a protecting gesture, covering Him with her veil, foreseeing the future—hearing the coarse voices of the money-changers, and seeing the sellers of holocaust in the Temple porticoes; perhaps she saw the shadow of

the Cross, of many crosses in the midst of the quarrelsome
shouting of those who denied Him and blasphemed.

In the realization of persecutions to come, she felt the
thrust of that sword point Simeon had foretold. Her destiny.
A sign of contradiction for Him: a piercing sword for her;
and whether in love or hate towards her, the thoughts of all
would be revealed. That sword, piercing her own soul asun-
der, would also divide the soul of humanity, splitting it in
two divisions—friends or enemies, love or hatred for her and,
therefore, for the fruit of her womb.

From that moment there would be those who loved her and
those who defamed her name; those who would give their
lives and their intelligence to proclaim her, and those who
would concoct calumnies against her and imagine heresies to
malign her, she who is eternally associated with the name of
her Son Jesus.

A few people had gathered around Joseph and Mary and
the old man Simeon. Among others who approached them
was Anna, a daughter of Phanuel of the tribe of Aser. She
was a widow eighty-four years old and had taken up her abode
in the house of the most High God, spending her days and
nights in prayers and fasting. She also expected the Messiah.
When she saw the Child her tired heart felt a thrill of joy.
Then she added her supplications to those of Simeon, an-
nouncing in the Temple entrances that the Messiah had
come.

The priests who listened shrugged their shoulders, judging
her definitely foolish. The money-changers behind their
counters winked at one another and sneered. The Messiah
they expected would come in gold ornaments, a bronze
breastplate, with arms and money; while the new-born Child
of this Galilean country girl seemed about to expire.

But it was time for them to leave the sacred precincts of
the Temple. Mary, now that the prophecy had clearly put be-

fore her mind all the impending evils, pressed her Son to her bosom in an agonizing gesture of tenderness. Probably she sought a secluded corner apart in the vestibule, a shelter where the animals waiting for sacrifice were put, in order to feed her Infant who was crying for His Mother's breast. She, with all the yearnings of her heart and her flesh, was happy to satisfy Him. In that act when life flowed in Him from her own life she forgot everything else. She heard again the music of Paradise and smiled on the innumerable invisible angels who lingered in loving flight to gaze tenderly upon them both. Joseph watched that scene that would so charm the human family: Jesus feeding at Mary's breast, which is also the feeding of reborn humanity.

Art and poetry did not finish for centuries, nor have they yet finished, representing this scene of innocent love; and for a long time theology has drawn nourishment from that same source.

Mary loved that flower of her flesh and blood of her blood as much as it is possible to love because in the caresses of her Child she recognized the embraces of God. She had generated Him Who had generated her, so her love was adoration; and she knew that He did not belong to her as much as she belonged to Him; while He, by love, belonged to men since He had chosen to be an offering for their salvation. She understood more and more clearly that His love would blossom into a bloody sorrow; and in her consciousness of this, although filled with anguish, this anguish was tempered with heroic strength through conforming her will to that of her Lord.

Gradually her motherhood was being extended to the whole mass of sinners who in the exchange of the Redemption would take the place of her Son. She was beginning already to suffer those spasms of pain coming to her in later days, and she offered herself; in her offering she was initiating her place as Co-Redemptrix.

Rising, Mary turned with Joseph towards the stone gate from which could be seen the mass of white houses that covered the hills. On one side was Herod's castle towering above the rest, guarded by foreign soldiers who stared at people with an insolent air. A little farther down, beyond the houses, on a desolate elevation, she saw three wooden poles fixed into the ground. Above them, around and around, flew shrieking black birds. She felt a clutch at her heart and clasped Joseph's arm.

"What are those black gibbets down there?" Joseph's heart sank and he shook his head.

"They are nothing. Do not look at them, woman!" And so they went on down the narrow streets among the bare-footed and shouting people who were carrying their baskets on their heads and urging on their donkeys. Squadrons of soldiers passed them. Their presence always reminded the Israelites that they were ruled by the Idumean Herod who lived in his barricaded castle with his wives and mistresses. Mary and Joseph stepped aside to let some Scribes and members of the Sanhedrim pass by, pompous and inflated with religiosity who were on their way to the Temple. They glanced with contempt, if they glanced at all, towards the two poor Galileans and their Infant. These Scribes and Pharisees, monopolizers of the Scriptures, the exclusive ones of religion, encased in their inward erudition and their outward arrogance, felt not the slightest inspiration when passing that little family whom some of the poor saluted with a gesture of the hand and a smile.

Mary sensed the atmosphere of hostile oppression which, like a dark wall, seemed to rise up from the midst of the people in that city. She was carrying the Son of God, but the people of God did not care and were unaware of it; in fact, they were preparing to resist Him. What the good old man Simeon had said, and the aged widow Anna, Mary's own intuition, aided by grace, made her clearly understand these prophecies; she felt sure that her walk through the streets of Jerusalem and the by-ways of Palestine was a journey towards sacrifice. So she accepted it for herself; and she accepted it for the little One in Whose eyes she discovered the ultra-human image of the Father, as though mirrored in a miniature pool in Paradise. How all these presentiments made her groan in the depths of her soul.

She leaned on Joseph's arm, and still more did she lean on the great Heart of God. So, brave but suffering, she went on with a sense of relief when they had passed out of the city gate into the open fields on their homeward way. As they walked, she exchanged a few words with Joseph to comfort him, for he had felt those shadows of the future which filled him with pain. While Joseph was thinking of the future of this Child, he suffered too, on account of Mary's sufferings. She kept all things in her heart as in a bitter reservoir of love, all she saw, all she heard, so that nothing was lost. Everything that concerned Jesus was vital, of life and death to her who was living for Him and with Him.

THE MAGI AND THE STAR

Back in Bethlehem once more, Mary witnessed another unexpected event. It was the adoration of her Child; not by the rough uncouth Jewish shepherds, but by three aristocratic, learned men from Iran who came from far away with a retinue of camels and servants. Six months previously they had started from their distant lands which lay between two great rivers. The apparition of a most unusual radiant star in the west had roused them from their studies in astronomy. They turned the pages of their ancient tomes; they consulted other learned men, but no hint or explanation of this constellation could be found. It was like a challenge of beckoning light calling them.

In their own country they knew from the Sacred Books
that a Saviour, born of a Virgin, would come into the world
at a period in time marked by an extraordinary appearance
of brilliant stars. Even the Semites in Arabia, perhaps due to
their contacts with the Hebrews and the Persians, knew these
Messianic prophecies. All such people, in a confused way,
awaited this Saviour, for everywhere the burden of sin was un-
bearable and with it came a yearning to be liberated; this
they instinctively felt when the promise was remembered. The
liberator was destined to fight the Devil and He would create
a regime of justice and peace, as the sage Zarathustra had
foretold.

Wherefore the three explorers, leaving the observations of
the stars and their oscillations, set out from Mesopotamia
(one of them may have been from Arabia) at the call of the
marvellous star. They turned their camels, heavily laden with
rich silk rugs, gifts and food, in the direction of the land
where the star pointed. Perhaps they all started together; perhaps they met on the way.

An ancient legend of the Middle Ages gives their names as
Gaspar, Melchior and Balthazar. Certainly they all three considered the heavenly signs worth leaving the comforts of home
and starting on a long and perilous journey. The distance did
not frighten them; rather, it seemed to invite them.

They crossed the desert of Syria, touched at Palmyra and
came to Damascus. Here they sought out the synagogue and
inquired if there the Messiah, the Expected One of Israel,
had come. They consulted with the Rabbis and the Sacred
Scriptures. From there they descended by the road that sloped
down to the right bank of the Jordan, stopping now and then
to strike camp, which the armed servants prepared and
guarded since the wilderness about them was infested with
roaming wolves and robbers.

Every night they noticed that the star increased in brilliancy and this made their hearts beat fast with anticipation. As time passed their desire to behold the Expected One burned more ardently. So one morning, just as the dawn was extinguishing the lights in the skies one by one, fading into a soft opalescence, they arrived in the sacred city of the Jews, led there by that star like a lamp in the heavens. Seated high on their swaying camels, the three wise men ascended the narrow stony streets, then up to the esplanade of the Temple. Here they dismounted and asked to speak with the priests.

"Peace be with you!" was their greeting. "Where is he that has been born, the king of the Jews? We have seen his star in the east and we have come to worship him."

The king of the Jews! The priests repeated these words to each other in a whisper, lest beyond those walls of stone Herod, the only king of the Jews, might hear and his bloody anger be aroused.

"The star? What star?" they asked.

None of the priests had seen it in that activity of celestial planets and stars which seem to swarm in the heavens at night above the houses and fields. Alas, they were too busy looking down on their smoky parchments to notice what was happening in the pure sky above them. However, since they were questioned by these personages of rank, as learned and majestic as kings, they gathered together to consult the Scriptures and to inquire of the Scribes.

Meanwhile the news of the arrival of the magnificent caravan had spread rapidly and had even reached the ears of Herod. That suspicious monarch was interested at once in the adventurous quest. These visitors were looking for no less a personage than a *king*. Herod's sleuths soon informed him; they were the first to be alarmed by that title. They knew how much bloodshed their master had required to secure that title against his rivals, with what jealousy he defended it against usurpers. If he were to lose it now, now when his

old legs trembled with age, the title would be passed on to a
son, perhaps to Archelaus. Who knows, it might be Antipas.
(Providing Herod did not strangle them, fearing they might
seize the title before their time). The truth is, he knew not
to whom to leave it, because he did not want to leave it at
all.

Therefore, when Herod heard the news, his languid and
stiffened arteries were filled with fury, but he did not let his
anger appear. He gave an order for the chief priests (his creatures whom he had gathered to serve him), also for the Scribes
and Elders, and without showing his agitation he inquired
secretly, "Where was it that Christ would be born?"

Then they repeated the Messianic prophecies, and made
Daniel's calculations, and found that the time had come and
Christ was about to be born, or was born, in Bethlehem, according to the prophecy of Micheas: "And thou, Bethlehem,
of the land of Juda, art far from the least among the princes
of Juda, for out of thee will arise a leader who is to be the
shepherd of my people Israel."

Herod knew now and needed no more explanations. He
had the Magi come to him privately to tell him more about
the star. Then meditating on the many crimes he had already
perpetrated in getting rid of rivals, he pretended to encour-
age them in their search.

"Go," he said, "and inquire carefully for the child, and
when you have found him, bring me back word, so that I too
may come and worship him." His voice was caressing, his
countenance expressed religious unction, and his long,
smooth beard, well pomaded, made him look like a grand old
priest.

The Magi obeyed him, and at night started out again, the
star reappearing in twinkling brilliance moving towards the
south, following a pathway never before made by any star.
They did not have far to go. Then they saw the star, trem-

bling with a sparkling smile, stop just above the village of Bethlehem, and from it a radiating delicate thread of light pointed directly down on a little house, hidden as were the others in the shadows of the night.

They stopped and waited, but it was not for long as the women of Palestine rise early to turn the mill-stone by the light of the stars. When the door of that little house opened the Magi asked respectfully if they might enter. Joseph admitted them and in the room they found the mother, with the Child in her arms, and she received them.

They fell on their knees and adored Him. Mary's eyes were filled with joy as she raised her arms in a sacrificial gesture to offer the Child born of her the better for their homage. In ecstatic joy they kissed His feet and the tiny hands that blessed them. Afterwards, the slaves brought in the chest and they offered their gifts. One offered jewels and gold, another offered incense, and the other offered myrrh. The mother observed these treasures and understood their significance with quick oriental intuition sharpened by her supernatural sensibility. She knew the symbolism of the gifts: the gold for a king, the incense for divinity, the myrrh for death. All the homage of these wise men of ancient times, as well as the homage of wise men of newer times, was a tribute of gratitude for the death the little King—a God—would meet for the salvation of mankind. There was always the vision of His death near the vision of His glory. He is the conqueror of death because He is the God of life.

Mary had said, "Behold the handmaid of the Lord; let it be unto me according to thy word." And saying this once more, she held out the Saviour of men, while her heart was weeping and from her breasts drops of milk fell like tears.

THE FIRST PERSECUTION

The first adoration offered the little King was from His mother and his foster father, Joseph, then the shepherds, and neighbors from among the country people. Next, two old people, Simeon and Anna living in the Temple, devoted entirely to the most High God; these represented Religion. Most people perceived nothing. Absorbed in amassing fortunes, their hearts yearned for nothing else. The priests themselves, who belonged to the very place of sacrifice, had observed nothing. Their minds were fixed on the red tape of government. Finally, strangers had come, the forerunners of those distant peoples who would run to meet the new faith with more enthusiasm and in larger numbers than those to whom it came. People would follow Him, passing over geographical and racial barriers, following the light of the star.

Thus the three Magi attained the purpose of all their years of astronomical study of the heavens, and prepared to return to their homes, ending their life's journey with the marvelous news, "The Saviour has come! We have seen Him with our own eyes. He was resting in the arms of His young mother."

But in the night before their departure, they received a warning not to go back to Herod. They understood and took leave of Mary and Joseph, bending low over the Divine Infant for the last time, while He waved His little hands joyfully towards their shining jeweled turbans. So they started as fast as they could by another road and left Herod's territory.

On the following night an angel appeared to Joseph and said, "Rise up, take with thee the child and his mother, and flee to Egypt; there remain, until I give thee word. For Herod will soon be making search for the child, to destroy Him."

Joseph leaped to his feet, much frightened. He understood at once the danger that threatened those two helpless creatures, the Child and His Mother who meant more to him than his life. From the very beginning Joseph had accepted his responsibility: a legal paternity over Jesus, and a bond with Mary which signified sacrifice, a running from place to place with a sword always over his head.

He awoke Mary and told her of the vision; then gathering their few household things together, some linens for the Child, the gifts of the Magi, some tools for his work which Joseph packed on the back of a donkey, they went silently and noiselessly out into the opaque night. It was the beginning of the persecution of the Church; it was the Church beginning her pilgrimage through the roads of a world that does not want her.

Joseph, like most Hebrews, knew the best places for crossing the frontier, as flight into Egypt was a common thing during the reign of the bloody Herod. But the country was small; so it was soon known at court that the Magi had slipped away. This irritated the despot's suspicions and he was more crudely fearful at the idea of a usurper than he was of the mysterious. Herod was the first representative of that political and antagonistic force which, out of jealous, suspicious fear of the supernatural royalty of Jesus, would subdue His religous power; and Herod gave to his future imitators the method by which to be rid of it—massacre.

He gave orders to kill all the men children born within the last two years in Bethlehem, presuming that among them would be the future king. He had perpetrated so many massacres that he could feel no qualms over the extermination of a few dozen infants still at the breast, and in a country district.

A pack of human bloodhounds fell upon the peaceful place. Closing all the roads to the fields and going from house to house, they stabbed the infants in their mother's arms. When there was resistance they killed the mothers; thus all the men children in Bethlehem of two years of age were put to death. For these bloodhounds of the king this was not a great slaughter; but for the mothers and fathers in this country district, at the sight of innocent blood immolated to the ferocity of a gouty despot, it was a scene of such horror and sorrow that it recalled to their memory other great national massacres. They remembered those exiled from Juda, and they thought they heard once more "Rachel weeping for her children, and she would not be comforted, because none is left."

Even now, every year, the Church weeps for them, overshadowing her joyful liturgy of Christmas. At the thought of that butchery, so innocently caused by her Child, Mary's heart must have nearly broken in her anguish. Those suckling infants with their frail bodies had sheltered the Saviour of the world, and their mothers were a protection to His mother. Innocence protecting the Innocent. It was intended thus so that men might bring their first contribution to the bloody sacrifice of Redemption.

All could have been accomplished by a miracle; but Divine Providence willed otherwise. God, having entered carnally among men, men should in some way merit that immense service by giving their work and their life, if needed. The Redemption became a part of their existence and influenced their affections; it was identified with their entire life and therefore became more precious.

That solidarity in which human beings harmonize the supernatural with the natural was beginning to act. If Jesus is the Reconciliator, then Mary being His mother, is Co-Reconciliatrix. St. Ephrem, who lived not long after her time, calls her this.

Here is another paradox: the King of the universe flees from a handful of assassins, hired for a few pennies, when with a mere gesture He could have destroyed them with their master so heavily laden with sin. Instead, He takes flight in the arms of a girl, escorted by a laborer, and accepting the protection of innocent blood. The paradox will be repeated many times, when innocent workmen and women will protect Christ in His Church, shielding Him with their persons and carrying Him away in the night; women will carry Him in their arms, and men with clean hearts will protect His flight in the nights of persecution and terror.

Joseph's soul must have been filled with a great confidence and humble pride because God had entrusted to him the honor of snatching the Son of God from death, and protecting the unparalleled mother. In Mary's heart and in the heart of the little Jesus, there welled up a great gratitude in the midst of fear for the chaste young man who was so willingly taking his part in the Divine Drama.

THE FLIGHT INTO EGYPT

Once more the plan of the Redemption was saved for Mary and Joseph, whose journeyings towards the hospitable land of idols have been dotted with legends by the piety of the redeemed. That sandy trail between the dunes and the sea has flowered into poetry again and again. It was imagined that weeping angels led the donkey by night over the clefts and brambles, hills and sand dunes, while Mary fed her Child. At every rustling of the leaves, at every moving of the shadows, she would hide Him under her mantle, her face pale with fear. For many a night she has covered with her mantle Christ pursued in His Church.

It is thought that at nightfall, and after three days of walking, the little party reached the border of the desert, black with shadows and the howling of hungry animals. At the sight of Mary's face, pale as death, pain clutched at Joseph's heart.

What could he do against that mysterious menace of limitless darkness?

They went on breathlessly, and behold, they came to a man's dwelling out of which two figures emerged, lifting a lantern to look at the faces of the two fugitives. Seeing the face of a young woman who held a child close in her arms, one of the brigands, the chief, grew pale and in an accent unusual for him, invited her to enter. He had a child in his house also, but for lack of some milk the babe was dying. Mary, with all the tender feelings of a mother, entered the dwelling and that night the child of the brigand nursed the Virgin's milk. What a wave of purity and warmth must have flowed through his tiny veins so stained with his parent's guilt.

When this child of the desert grew up and became a brigand like his father, he seemed to have a mixture of goodness, a little warmth in him, given him from the milk of the Madonna. A little more than thirty years later, he fell into the hands of the Roman police. Then as he hung on a cross beside Jesus, his hard spirit, tainted with the blood of murderers, was also tainted with the goodness of long ago. This goodness awoke in him, and he turned to Jesus as his father had one day turned to Mary. And Jesus drew him as His half-brother into heaven, after having made him his real blood relation with His own precious Blood.

It was Jesus Who had taken Mary so far; brought her in contact with highway robbers, then idolators in Egypt and later with publicans and sinners. She, the all-pure, brought purity into contact with impurity; Redemption into the midst of slavery. This assiduous offering of salvation was her proper duty wherever she found decay.

Urging the donkey on, they followed the trail along the seashore. During the day the sea looked like shining metal, but it roared wildly, far surpassing the tiny sea of Galilee near Nazareth which at that moment seemed so far away, quite beyond their reach. After ten days of march along the scorched plains and across the desert, they reached Egypt, and there they wandered, asking for lodging in the houses of the poor. Finally, they found a resting place, probably at Heliopolis, near some community of Israelites; several groups of whom lived in those surroundings.

THE FUGITIVES IN EGYPT

The life of the Holy Family (like a family of emigrants, or a small group of Church refugees) has not been recorded, but it is quite possible to imagine it. Theirs was the life of all refugees who have no goods; who live between the fear of police at home or abroad; outlawed, and obliged to hide themselves among anonymous stratas of poor people so as not to be suspected or found. The two from Galilee probably lived on alms, or loans at small interest, and by humiliations. Mary fed her Child, king of the world, at her pure breast. Just to look at Him was Paradise for her: living within the sphere of the miraculous, Joseph worked from house to house, helping out some carpenter, and earning enough to buy a little flour or pay for the use of some humble dwelling in the outskirts of the city where the larger buildings dwindle to musty huts on dusty, neglected by-ways. Heaven's purity was the guest of earth's sordid poverty.

But they did not remain long in exile, for an angel appeared one night to the tired carpenter in his sleep and said, "Rise up, take with thee the Child and His mother, and return to the land of Israel; for those who sought the Child's life are dead."

Full of joy, Joseph lifted up the Child, awoke His mother

(neither the angel nor the Scriptures ever say Joseph's "wife," but "the Child and His mother," for Mary's function was just that) and gathering together the few things they owned, he led them back to Galilee.

The Mother
of the Family

Beautiful Jesus, sweet Jesus, be a brother to me.
Beautiful maiden, comely maiden, so worthy of honor.
Joyful maiden, most admirable and fruitful to God
Make me strong in overcoming spiritual death;
Take away my fear, take away eternal pain.[1]

THE HOUSEKEEPER

After the exhausting heat of the desert and the monotonous plains, Mary and Joseph gazed with tears of joy at the distant hills that outlined the confines of their own country. They heard from the first fellow-countrymen whom they met of the tragic death of the cruel king who had spent his last months, as he had his whole life, between conspiracies and poisonings. The old vulture, who counted his days by his crimes, had resisted to the end, with his iron claws, all attempts at uprisings. He had ordered burned alive forty young men. He had judged them guilty of beheading the golden eagle which he had, in an idolatrous way, placed against the Temple. Feeling his bowels burning within him, worms eating him alive and despairing of recovery, Herod gathered together all the

[1] Pulcher Jesus, dulcis Jesus, sis mihi frater.
Pulchra puella, venusta puella, puella colenda,
Virgo incunda Deoque fecunda nimisque stupenda,
Fac me fortem vincere mortem spiritualem,
Tolle timorem, pelle dolorem perpetualem.
A.H. 32,127.

71

chief governors in the country for a great feast in the Hippo-
drome, and here, as soon as he expired, they would be butchered so that tears for them would drown the joy felt over his
death. At the last, just before he died, he had another one of
his sons, Antipater put to death.

Philip and Antipas succeeded him with the title of te-
trarchs, and Archelaus with the title of king of Judea. Archelaus initiated his reign with the massacre of three thousand
citizens gathered in Jerusalem for the Feast of the Azymes; at
least, he showed himself in cruelty a worthy son of his father.

Mary listened with deep emotion to all this news while
caressing the locks of the Child Jesus Who was now beginning
to take His first steps and to play with other little ones His
own age; perhaps the younger brothers of the martyred Inno-
cents who, looking at Him for the first time, stared at Him
with wide inquisitive eyes. Then gazing into the limpid
depths of His own they drew near with faltering steps, attracted by His smiling sympathy.

Joseph had quickly gathered enough of the news to realize
that the air of Judea was not for them. At the first suspicion
Archelaus would have repeated the deed of his father Herod.
And although the little family was much exhausted, they went
straight to Galilee (where Antipas was tetrarch) and finally
reached Nazareth. Their few poor relatives who were still
there were glad to see them again and gave them a helping
hand in clearing out one of the caves in the hillside, where
Joseph could settle his family and assemble the few tools of
his trade.

The ordinary life of every man, as it did for Joseph, began
with the struggle for his daily bread. Mary drew to herself the
hearts of her two dear ones and of others among her relations
far and near; she welcomed them all as they gathered about
her lively Child Who played at fashioning tiny crosses on
His father's work bench. If He went out of doors to play with

some of His little companions, He could not resist bringing them into the house to share with them the sight of His mother; that was a joy which grew more delightful every day.

She worked without sparing herself in order to keep her house and to help Joseph. She turned the millstone, carried the water (probably from the fountain called even to this day "the Virgin's fountain"). She washed, cooked, swept and sewed; all the tired labor that was wearing out her physical strength became a service of adoration for her Son, as well as the result of her motherly love.

The little contemplative whom the Archangel Gabriel had found absorbed in prayer, remained still united to God because always united in a visible manner with her Son. Praying, she looked at those golden locks, that delicate, although strong, little body, moving from one duty of prayer to the other of work. Her divine maternity brought pain at every moment.

Her Son, when He could, helped her and Joseph, making Himself useful. Especially at night when people rested from their labors, and on the Sabbath in the synagogue, He attracted everyone by His concentration in prayer and meditations of the Scriptures. The questions He asked, the remarks and comments with which He illustrated His narratives astonished everyone but first of all His mother, who was quick to see in every allusion some confirmation of the prophecies and her own presentiments relating to the Redemption through His blood.

Often her heart bled with anguish; because, through her Child as Redeemer, all others born of women would benefit by that Redemption to whom the blood of Jesus (her blood) would give salvation. She felt that she had born them to eternal life and they were forever hers. Her heart was the heart of the mother of all the living. To her heart, as to a haven of peace, came all the anxious requests for help, all the aspirations of crowds of desperate people, and from the souls of solitaries in every language, under the stars everywhere; sad and weary ones dragging themselves along through life with their burden of sin and failing strength.

THE HOLY FAMILY

This was the Holy Family; the poorest, most modest, most silent family in that miserable village, Nazareth. Poetry and art have tried to depict the family living under the canopy of blue skies, a background of green hills, smiled upon by the sun, a flock of doves flying overhead. There may have been doves, since the birds of the air and the animals of the earth instinctively tried to get near the source of life. But with the doves, there were hawks also, and in the lower strata of creatures, wasps and vipers.The people of Nazareth sneered with knowing airs at the three absorbed in work and prayer. Those who lorded it over the rest were quite willing to annoy and lay snares for Joseph. When evening came and relatives were gathered in the little house, they urged Joseph to retaliate or obtain justice for himself. The strong descendant of King David, always just, only shook his head, looking at Mary and her Son. If the argument became heated, Mary's eyes would brim with tears of pity, and the Boy Jesus with accents of rightful authority would interfere and cut the discussion short.

"We must forgive! Forgive, not once, but seventy times seven."

The old people looked at Him with surprise and grumbled, as much as to say, "We can understand nothing of today's youth." Jesus bewildered and confused them with those ideas of love which Mary tolerated, so they growled in their tangled beards. They were thinking of other boys whose thoughts were full of vengeance towards strangers; this One thought too much of the Israelites and the prophets.

The Holy Family! There were some who looked at the little family group as at a model, there were others who hated them. The good were drawn to them with a sweet sympathy: the evil and passionate drew away from them.

In the village factions were continually forming of the irritable, the discontented and the avaricious people against those three who, although poor and vexed by misfortune, still had the courage to keep smiling, always ready to help everybody, always praying. Some people only saw in them cause for reproach and, when they could, they gave vent to their feelings by fabricating calumnies against Mary. They knew only good could be said about her, and they accused Joseph of wrong-doing, although he was "the just man" par excellence. They imputed deeds of violence to that Boy who was the friend of all children.

Jesus pacified them when they came to blows in the games. When they chased one another down the steep streets, like stairs and, slipping, fell in a heap in the mud, pommeling each other, he picked them up as they wiped their eyes with the back of their dirty hands. He led them by the hand to His mother—His own, therefore, theirs too, that she might comfort them with soothing words; and getting a basin of water and a bit of fresh fruit, their tears soon gave place to joy. When they left Mary's house, their eyes shone like twin stars newly washed in dew.

If He met older boys or men in the village square who quarreled or spoke evil words, He gently rebuked them with a word of Scripture or shamed them with a look.

Whether in the natural or the supernatural order the Holy Family is the model for all families. Consecrated virgins look at the trio, who are all three virgins, as their exemplar, since religious too have given their flesh in the service of the Redemption. Parents look at the three as the perfect family, united in labor and love; where the workshop was transformed into a temple, and family life became a liturgy. They are a unique family, even in the details of ordinary living they spent almost all the time in silence.

Joseph was the "just" man described in the Old Testament. All his thoughts, acts of family government, and his work were for the glory of God, according to the spirit of the Mosaic Law; to the workman whose work was well done it was a matter of conscience, so that excellency in handiwork was the proof of an honest soul. The life of Joseph, as head of the family, was consumed in the service of his own. He had a unique sense of the deep veneration due the woman and an ecstatic adoration for the Boy. Joseph was the believer, leaning on God, and in the service he gave he expected nothing, hoped for nothing, feared nothing from the world which he looked upon as merely the scene of the great Messianic drama, the unfolding of which the Almighty would bring about in His own way.

And the Woman! If Joseph personified justice, she was the incarnation of purity. On the part of humanity, she *was* purity.

"O flower of Chastity, thou art sustained by love."

In the long rainy seasons the interior of that cave became damp and musty, mud from the dirty streets was swept down to the entrance. Mary's hands, calloused from work, seemed to brighten everything they touched; wherever her eyes rested, there was light; when she spoke, the air became radiant. No ignoble thought was possible in her presence. She was as comely as the first creation before its Fall; beautiful as she was, coming from the Creator, her beauty did not stir up dark passions but put to flight evil thoughts. Her purity penetrated the conscience like a sword of fire and enkindled in others good and holy thoughts. When she was seen walking along the

*Fathers
and Doctors
of the Church
Write about
Mary*

OUR LADY OF THE HOLY SPIRIT — *F. Nagni*
The Son of God did not choose for His Mother some rich or wealthy noble, but rather that Blessed Virgin whose soul was so rich in virtue. This blessed woman, Mary, conceived Christ in her womb because she preserved her chastity above all of human nature.

St. John Chrysostom

THE NATIVITY — *F. Nagni*
When we attempt to understand the mystery of the Nativity of Christ,
Who was born of a Virgin Mother, the mists of earthly reason must be
banished and the smoke of mundane wisdom must be swept from eyes
illuminated by faith.   St. Leo

MOTHER AND CHILD — *F. Nagni*
The Mediator between God and man, from the very instant of His birth
joins the Divine and the human, the highest and the lowest. He is born
of a woman, but in such a way that the flower of her virginity is not
harmed in any way by motherhood.   ST. BERNARD

JESUS AND MARY — *E. Giaroli*

We certainly should not be surprised that God, Who is blessed and wonderful in His saints, should be yet more marvelous in His *Mother*. Virgins may praise the motherhood of this Virgin; the married may honor the virginity of this Mother. All men can imitate the humility of the Mother of God.   ST. BERNARD

MOTHER AND SON — *P. Morbiducci*

Mary, recognizing her position as His Mother, did not hesitate to call Him "Son" whom the angels serve in reverence. Nor did God hesitate to respond to the name and to revere the maternal Majesty He had bestowed on her.   St. Bernard

THE PIETÁ — *E. Manfrini*

O truly Blessed Mother, the sword has pierced. The only way it could cut was to see the piercing of your Divine Son. After He had breathed His last, when the cruel sword could not touch His Spirit as it passed through His side, surely it pierced your own soul.   St. Bernard

THE ASSUMPTION — *N. Cassino*
Among all the feasts that have been celebrated through the centuries, the Feast of the Assumption is one of the greatest. Emmanuel entered the world as a stranger, but you received Him into yourself as into a palatial manor. Today you are received by Him into the regal palace of Heaven, to have Him bestow on you the place of honor, worthy of the Mother of such a Solomon.   St. Peter Canisius

CORONATION OF THE VIRGIN — *F. Nagni*

Happy the day on which the most humble of handmaidens is raised to her position as Queen of Heaven and most powerful Mistress of the world. No higher position is possible in her Son's Kingdom. Her throne is next to Christ's in glory.　　　　　　　　Sᴛ. Pᴇᴛᴇʀ Cᴀɴɪsɪᴜs

MOTHER OF THE AFFLICTED — *F. Nagni*

Mary ardently desires that not a single soul perish whom her Son has redeemed by His precious Blood in His saving death.

St. Robert Bellarmine

MEDIATRIX OF GRACE — *F. Nagni*

The grace of God, so necessary to heal mankind, is dispensed to us through Mary. As from an aqueduct, grace flows through Mary. What her Son won by strict right, Mary dispenses as a most merciful Queen, compassionating her needy people.　　　Sᴛ. Bᴏɴᴀᴠᴇɴᴛᴜʀᴇ

STAR OF THE SEA — *F. Nagni*
When you find yourself tossed by the raging storms on the great sea
of life, far from land, keep your eyes fixed on this Star to avoid disaster.
When the winds of temptation or the rocks of tribulation threaten, look
up to the Star, call upon Mary!   ST. BERNARD

MADONNA — *F. Nagni*

Christ was a virgin and His mother was ever-virgin. His mother is a
closed garden, a sealed fountain. From the fountain flow rivers of
water, says the prophet Joel, to wash away ropes and thorns. The ropes
are the sins that hold us down. The thorns are the cares that stifle
the good seed.   St. Jerome

THE VIRGIN — *F. Nagni*

"Do not be afraid, Mary, for you have found grace." How true this is!
Whoever finds grace has nothing to fear and "You have found Grace."
O Blessed Virgin who alone merited to hear these words before any
other of our race, "You have found Grace."   Sᴛ. Pᴇᴛᴇʀ Cʜʀʏsᴏʟᴏɢᴜs

MARY, MOTHER OF GOD, — *F. Nagni*
Truly you are blessed among all women because, while remaining a
woman, a creature of our race, you have become the Mother of God.

ST. SOPHRONIUS

dusty roads with a pitcher of water on her head, even the boldest boys hushed their shouts.

She passed by, absorbed in her thoughts which were not of this world; if she lifted her eyes ever so little a mysterious wave of something divine, like an intimate desire to mend one's ways, seemed to penetrate the souls of those who saw her. She was the natural intermediary between the Son and Joseph. Joseph, so fully conscious of everything in the Law, was often astonished at the discourses of Jesus, and Mary would soften his surprise with her love. She did likewise with relatives and friends by preparing their minds to understand Jesus. Since she was full of grace, she clothed all her words with grace, which convinced those who listened to her.

Already at Nazareth, she stood between the old world and the new, between the Old Law that was dying and the New Law established between Jesus and men. Kneeling on a mat or sitting with some work in hand, she abandoned her soul to God, conscious of that ocean of sin that seemed daily pressing at her door and pouring in like a great burden to rest at her feet; then an infinite pity would consume her in a desire to hasten the time of universal Purification.

She, the mother of the Saviour (the instrument of man's salvation), was mindful of all those unfortunate ones moving so rapidly towards death with the heavy burdens of hatred, impurity and covetousness in their souls. Pure, she wished to see all these souls become pure as lamb's wool, white like the snow of the hills. Then she would draw her Son to her side and in silence place herself between Him and that threatening crowd; hastening the moment of reconciliation when love would circulate again from the Creator to the creature, passing through her heart first as through a filter.

Jesus—Divinity Incarnate—stood between Mary and Joseph. He was the Son of God made flesh. And yet, nothing distinguished Him from other boys in the eyes of the super-

7. *Nazareth*

ficial. His features were more beautiful than those of others (He had His mother's features) and He was physically perfect. He was also poorer than other children, had more to endure than they, and His home, precisely because it was *His* home, was constantly the target of evil. Although those three holy ones forgave, prayed and smiled, they often wept; the wicked pressed and vexed them; nature, used by the Devil, assailed them. They knew many hours of anxiety and days without bread. The tax gatherers assailed them, thieves stole from them, and they saw sickness bereave them of dear ones.

In fact, there was no peaceful living in Herod's regime among people goaded with misery. And yet Jesus grew as straight as a flower in the midst of aggression which seemed to press in on Him as though to bend Him down. He grew as straight as a stem reaching up to His Father in heaven. It is not believable that His evangelization only began when He was thirty years old. He only *initiated* it at the age of thirty for people outside His home. He was revealing it to Mary and Joseph day by day; revealing the new economy of the Kingdom which grew with His natural growth. His relatives were often amazed, and even stupified; thus the expressions of their confusion were often circulated among others of their kinsfolk. Up to this time, His family was the Kingdom of God on earth. It was the Church in miniature.

The Church composed of justice, purity and divinity, united and one in charity, like that little house, began to permeate a world wherein iniquity, lust and idolatry had created a prison, and where terror and hatred blew like a howling hurricane.

SEEKING JESUS

No remarkable event happened in those years. At least the canonical gospels do not record any. The apocryphal gospels tell of some imaginary happenings.

The little family went to the fields for the sowing, for the reaping and for the harvest. From the memory of these events, Jesus was to draw many of His parables in explaining to the multitudes the Kingdom of God, which would be a growth tended by the Divine Husbandman.

In the quiet existence in that village, a visit to Jerusalem was a great event and people would prepare for it a long time ahead. Jerusalem was the holy city to which Israelites turned often in their hearts and to which they returned in person from every corner of three continents at least once a year. It was like a great "rally" or reunion of a dispersed people. God was in Jerusalem, in the one great Temple, where there was the one legal altar of sacrifice. The great prophets had been killed in Jerusalem and their blood had made the city a sacred place.

To Jesus, the Temple was the house of His Father; as it was also to His mother. With one heart they returned there especially for the Pasch. They would leave the cave, fastening the door with a big stick. Their food they loaded on a donkey or carried on their shoulders and, joining others, they started for the place destined in the designs of God to be the scene of the greatest Act: the point where the Divine Plan entered into human living. There in Jerusalem would be raised a pole which would replace the Temple soon to be devoured by flames, the great altar for the one great Sacrifice for all people.

In the Temple the three pilgrims expressed their devotion by their own intimate effusions of love; it was a family love. The Divine Boy told the Father of the deep love that prompted Him to take human form, in a rank of creatures despised and destined to bring such tremendous humiliation and failure. The mother humbled herself in adoration to the Father, at the same time rejoicing most intimately in her union with her Spouse, the Holy Ghost, whose fruit was at her side. Joseph in his humility was asking why God had chosen him, a poor carpenter, to represent Him, the Heavenly Father, on earth, and why the greatest mystery of divine love was lived in so much poverty. Adoring the designs of Heaven, Joseph would give thanks and from the depths of his simplicity accept his obedience.

Their prayers were associated and interwoven with those thousands of fellow-Jews who forgot before the altar of the Living God all the injuries they had endured coming along the roads of the Empire from Arabia and Persia. Once more they rose up with renewed hope and pride in being a united people, forgetting their miserable struggle for existence in the midst of pagans, exposed as they were, every day, to the temptation of avarice and to compromise with the idolatry about them.

It was in one of these pilgrimages, after the ceremonies were over, that Mary and Joseph started their homeward journey, in the belief that the Boy Jesus was in the returning caravan with either relatives and friends or with boys of his own age. Like all boys of all times, the boys of Nazareth, in the novelty of the feast and the enchanting sights of the city, took more steps than the grown-ups and followed those who went faster. They walked in groups and sang and told stories continually. The world of the youngsters is not that of their fathers nor yet wholly that of their mothers. They love to form in ranks holding one another by the shoulders, then suddenly break ranks to climb some high crag or run down to some well; to step aside to let a wedding procession pass, or a flock of sheep.

When evening came and they made their first stop, the families reassembled to eat, to rest and to sleep. Mary and Joseph waited for Jesus to rejoin them. At that hour all the children sought out their own families as little chickens creep under the wings of the mother hen. Jesus always showed His happiness in His loving eyes whenever He returned to His mother.

That evening He did not come. His mother's anxiety increased rapidly, although Joseph tried to reassure her. They decided to begin the search at once.

Relatives and acquaintances were questioned. At each negative reply Mary's grief deepened. In vain her friends tried to console her. She stepped quickly, she inquired with insistence, and soon her voice was filled with tears. The company of the caravan saw her running along the return road towards the holy city. Her breathless sobs could be heard in the darkness that was descending from the stars; and from time to time the barking of dogs and the voice of shepherds filled the stillness.

"JESUS! JESUS!"

In the mother's cry all mankind was echoing, "Jesus! Jesus!" During the dark nights of Christianity, fearing the loss of the Saviour the call of grief will be heard, "Jesus! Jesus!" That name of love will become a cry of anguish, a cry of loss, calling the Eternal back to this black earth.

At dawn Mary and Joseph were back in Jerusalem exhausted from their long walk and loss of sleep. Jerusalem was a city packed with people. It was a labyrinth of ascending and descending narrow streets and small houses piled one on top of the other, somewhat like a disorderly troop storming the Acropolis. In that labyrinth Mary and Joseph went from door to door asking their questions. To all their acquaintance and to all the places where Jesus might have gone, they went, trying to imagine where He might be. Some had seen Him, or thought they had, offering their suggestions to the two distracted ones seeking Him.

At every turn new human ant-hills appeared; from them laughing children, grumbling old women and quarreling pedlars came and went. Mary and Joseph climbed to the top of the city and then descended to the poorest section once more; it was all in vain. The longer the end of their quest was delayed, the greater grew their anxiety, like a fever heightened by forebodings.

In her suffering the poor mother took no food, accepted no comfort, for that Child was her life, and the thought of Him tormented her as she thought of the snares and mysterious dangers that surrounded Him under those low arched walls and treacherous turns in that wicked labyrinth.

But Love can do all things and Love took Mary and Joseph through that jungle of dark narrow streets regardless of their extreme fatigue. After three days' search, they were passing in front of the many halls grouped near together in the precincts of the Temple, when they heard the voice of a youth. *His voice* recognizable from any other. His voice coming from the midst of a crowd of bearded rabbis.

With palpitating hearts Mary and Joseph made a passage for themselves through the crowd which moved with bad grace to let the two Galileans go by. They were peasants, ignorant of the Law, on whom the Scribes and Pharisees showered much contempt. Mary and Joseph were filled with wonderment at the scene that met their eyes. The Boy was seated on a stool, listening to the most learned teachers. He questioned them and answered their questions. His answers were given in a clear voice and were as clear in wisdom. The group of argumentative controversialists were listening to Him with amazement, pleased and yet fearful. They had never seen or heard anything like this before.

When there was a pause in the exchange of questions and answers, the mother drew near and expressed herself in words most gentle and loving as only a mother can speak. They were a sweet reproach, at the same time, a sorrowful expression of her love and pain.

"My Son, why hast thou treated us so? Think what anguish

of mind thy father and I have endured, searching for thee."

Then the Boy gave one of those answers that was like a dark cloud pressing down upon her heart, a cloud coming up out of the future flecked with blood.

"What reason had you to search for me? Could you not tell that I must needs be in the place which belongs to my Father?"

Mary and Joseph did not understand. Here was something they could not grasp, which eluded Mary's comprehension too. In His words there was something intrinsically divine concerning the union of the Son with the Father; the mystery of Christ's presence in the world: something outside the range of the human. However, this was not the time for explanations, but for suffering.

Jesus was asking for another renunciation, the renunciation of blood and human affection as an offering for His divine mission. Mary must give all, even the love for her Son, for the sake of His mission—His love for the Father and for men. In other words she was asked to open her heart wide in universal love for all men, at this moment offering for it her only Son.

Thus she gave Him to us little by little. And in her giving she gave herself. Jesus had now initiated His mission. He began by teaching. Mary would continue in her mission which would be all of suffering.

The three returned to Nazareth, filled with the mystery of this first manifestation of Jesus as a teacher to men who were to learn from Him. Mary gathered all the details of this happening to keep them safe in her memory.

Let it be noted here that Jesus, having affirmed His Father's rights, obeyed His mother and followed her home. This is a sign that the mother's will could not differ from the Father's will, but formed one will with it. St. Luke, the Evangelist, relating these facts which no doubt he received from Mary herself, said, "He went down with them on their journey to Nazareth, and lived there in *subjection* to them."

Except in the case of a direct order from the Heavenly Father, the will of God was represented for Jesus by His parents on earth—His mother and foster-father. Obedience to God is broader than obedience to men, and one does not oppose the other. It is the same obedience but of growing dimensions. The obedience of the God-Man to two creatures is not a lost lesson; it elevates parental authority to the dignity of the divine and gives a clear model of dependence to children, which leads them in a continual growth in grace and wisdom.

THE DEATH OF JOSEPH

One day Jesus' obedience was narrowed down to obedience to Mary His mother, for Joseph slept in the Lord. His passing was the most beautiful of all the patriarchs, for it took place in the arms of the Son of God by Whom he was obeyed, and of the Mother of God by whom he was venerated. Perhaps it was fatigue that wore out his constitution, or some malady that entered the blood stream, or some accident that cut him off in the midst of his work. Calamities were frequent in those days among the poor. Whatever may have been the cause, it formed a part of God's plan. Since Jesus was now almost grown to manhood, legal protection was no longer necessary, and the time had come when only Jesus and His mother would remain on the scene of the Redemption. Later, she too, would withdraw from sight.

Joseph's part, like that of Mary, was made up of humility and service. This done, he disappeared. For a long time he remained hidden in the life of the Church herself, letting the figures of his dear ones, Jesus and Mary, blossom first in her worship; then he too would ascend after them, as formerly when returning from Egypt he could be seen mounting the hills, followed by the woman who advanced like a queen carrying the King of the world in her arms.

Surely death, coming to that good worker in his poor dwelling, brought great pain to Joseph as he thought of her who would be a widow and the Boy who was now deprived of support. The resigned look in the eyes of Mary comforted him, as did the words of divine faith which Jesus whispered to him.

Joseph's death was, in all reality, a loss to the two who were left. He had been an indefatigable worker, providing his own with all they needed. He said very little; but he was filled with the spirit of God which he drew from the Scriptures, and from Jesus and Mary. His task was a daily service for the good of the two persons entrusted to him, and he had done it well. Moreover he knew who they were. He knew the kind of woman Mary was, and what kind of boy Jesus was. He served them with veneration and adoration. No one had loved the things of God with such purity of soul as Joseph. His love for Mary was only a brief pause in his unique love for the Father, coming to rest in Mary's heart in order to pass on, purified, into the heart of Jesus; a love unfolding and completing itself between the two persons most worthy of love.

Now, cut down in the vigor of his mature manhood, he lay on a mat in the center of the bare room that was kitchen, workshop and bedroom for the little family. Relatives came to comfort Mary; and to recall the great patience, the toil, the gentleness of Joseph in whose veins ran the blood of the noblest of kings. And they raised long, shrill lamentations over him, while intimate friends wrapped his body in a winding sheet sprinkled with spices. Then before nightfall, they carried him to the common burial grounds outside the village, while the two persons most dear to him followed, weep-

ing. The people, who met them on the way and joined the
cortège, exclaimed with surprise because Mary and her Son,
although weeping, did not tear their garments or give any
outward signs of despair. As if death were not death for
them!

When night had fallen on the hills, they returned. The
relatives had gone, and the poor room appeared more lonely
than ever. Mary felt her loss bitterly; crossing her arms on
Joseph's work bench and resting her head upon them, she
wept. She wept for Joseph, her faithful companion and
trusted confidant, a brother as chaste as the angels, until her
wonderful Son, Who let her give vent to her sorrow, caressed
her hair, called her by name and whispered into her ear under her veil, "Mother!" Then he knelt in front of her and
spoke words to her, the greatest, no doubt, ever spoken from
the brink of death by the Author of Life. His love and His
revelations were a sweet orientation to the widow's sorrow, so
well understood in the light of her motherly love. From that
moment her solicitude for Him doubled, and she felt the
obligation of supplementing Joseph's care with her own.

From then on existence progressed along the line of sacrifice. If life had been hard before, it was harder now; it became rough because in the whole of ancient society the condition of a widow was the most unfortunate. A widow was a
sort of socially abandoned person, against whom life's miseries, the greediness of far too many, the hatred of relatives,
together with the lack of consideration in the Law and customs, all combined to bear down upon her like stormy waves
beating upon the remnants of a ship wreck.

From then on Mary had to work harder than ever. Her Son
took Joseph's place, but she spared Him as much as she could,
fearing a thousand dangers. She did not wish Him to work
alone in the mountains or stay too long in the fields. He re-
sponded to her solicitude in many loving ways. Meanwhile,

as He daily worked with His tools, He was preparing His plan for the distribution of His message, which we call the Gospel.

In the evening hours He and His mother had long, long talks while she spun her wool, wove or mended. Often other young people of Galilee came to listen, and Jesus tried to convince them that the interests of God held first place and had precedence over the task of gathering together a fortune. Frequently He went away during the day to continue these conversations.

Once He went to the banks of the Jordan river to be baptized by John, son of Elizabeth, Mary's aged relative. On that occasion a manifestation of the Spirit of God had revealed something of His personality to those present. After this, friends became His followers, and even some of John's disciples joined Him. A group of young people, loving God's glory, began to follow the young Nazarene, entering upon a heroic adventure with all the enthusiasm of youth.

Mary at Cana

These manifestations of ardent Galilean youth gathering around her Son, Mary permitted, and rejoiced on account of their active dedication to the things of God. Nevertheless, she felt some trepidation of soul for the risks it involved in a world that wanted to hear of God only with moderation. Meanwhile, she redoubled her labors so that Jesus should lack for nothing. One day there came to Mary and Jesus and their nearest relatives an invitation to a wedding in Cana. Very probably the bridegroom was related to Mary, or he may have been one of those who had listened to Jesus. In fact, the invitation was extended, not only to Jesus, but also to His disciples. Perhaps it was from Nathaniel, a native of Cana, who wished to see his young Master and His disciples there. It was a real charity to accept the invitation because one would bring a gift for the bride and in this way help in supplying the needs of the household. By accepting the invitation they would increase the number of guests in a celebration which was often the only bright spot for these people in the gray days of their existence. As a rule, the rich refused to sit at table with villagers, thus the poor used to celebrate the feast with people like themselves.

Early in the morning,[1] Mary and her Son with His young followers went up the mountain. She hurried a little to keep pace with them, while they retarded their steps and their exuberance for her sake. Jesus was now thirty years old and, as His mother had ever been, chaste and pure. He had never had any thought of marriage for Himself, living with His mother on earth and His Father in Heaven, contented with His poverty and His work.

Mary, although not much advanced in age, but showing the signs of her hard struggle with the exigencies of life which rapidly wears out a woman in the Orient, now walked with signs of fatigue, and in the steeper places she leaned on the arm of her Son. He was full of attention for her. His companions were happy to be with Him and with the woman who had given them the Messiah, the hope and pride of Hebrew youth. In the eyes of the country folk coming down the road, urging on their beasts of burden, those two were merely other working people of Galilee. But when they looked attentively into the deep and limpid eyes of the young Nazarene, and at the dovelike serenity of the Nazarene woman, they received a sudden illumination, an inspiration that stirred their souls, and they would salute the two in the name of God as they passed on.

When the little party arrived at their destination and had

---

[1] It is not clear from St. John 1:1,2 whether Mary was already in Cana before the wedding, to help the bride in her preparations, or if the invitation sent to her was also extended to Jesus and His followers.

presented their good wishes to the groom, they joined the other guests; then all together the entire company went to the house of the bride. She, adorned with cheap jewels and wearing the nuptial wreath, came forward, smiling with flushed cheeks, from the midst of her relatives and friends. Thus the wedding procession formed. Preceded by musicians and escorted by frolicsome little boys, it wended its way through the streets of the town to the house of the bridegroom. Here the banquet took place.

At the dinner, sheep from the flock were eaten along with fruits of the soil, both seasoned with a cheer re-enforced by good wine. It is not to be thought for a moment that Jesus and His mother took part in the meal with the aloofness of the Sadducees, afraid to contaminate themselves. On the contrary, they shared in it with sincere hearts, enjoying everything freely with the newly wedded ones and with the other guests. They entered into the spirit of the feast for, in it, two lives were united into one by a miracle of God. Their faces revealed no dark looks, and if some guests, less refined, checked some unseemly remarks, it was not for lack of mirth but because of the presence of those two persons who radiated innocence and dissipated with a glance the least unbecoming thought.

Now, as the company ate, alternating between compliments to the bride and quips of fun to the groom, the wine, which the two families had saved for years and which guests had brought, suddenly gave out. The guests at table were more numerous than had been expected; there were the musicians, the gate-keepers, the neighbors, and many others, all of whom had been drinking wine in the kitchen; besides, the long walk, the talking and laughter had sharpened everyone's thirst.

Of course the invited guests did not notice what had happened. But she who observed everything, who cared for the

happiness of others with a mother's heart, Mary of Nazareth—
she was aware of it and immediately concerned. This was like
her. Wherever there was privation, it became hers. She lived
for others: for her Son's brothers—her sons. What was to be
done in such an emergency?

In a village of scanty resources it was not easy to find wine
at a moment's notice; there may not have been any money to
pay for it. In the meantime, the guests might have discovered
the fact, felt badly or shown their surprise by sarcastic looks
or remarks; while the young couple would have been sadly
embarrassed, all their happiness spoiled, while the bright
memory of their wedding would have a shadow cast over it
for years. There was need for prompt intervention above the
ordinary.

Mary knew her Son. He was the Son of God. The miracle
of creating wine where wine was not, He alone could perform.
So she bent towards Him and whispered, "They have no
wine!"

She said only that; but she meant especially, above everything else, "You alone can provide it."

His mother suddenly presented Jesus with the occasion of
performing a public miracle; an occasion for manifesting
His divine mission to the world, for beginning that public
career which would end on a gibbet.

Jesus, wrapped in His reserve as Son of God, replied, "Nay,
woman, why dost thou trouble me with that? My time has
not come yet." Evidently to Jesus and to His mother, the
small affair of the failing wine cannot be of such interest
as to cause the unfolding of the mystery of Redemption:—
yet, both facts are for the glory of God.

In Oriental usage, the name "woman" is one of honor. As
Jesus used it, He addressed her with a kind of solemnity and
a sense of detachment. She, on the contrary, was not at all disturbed, knowing that her Son would obey her. Apparently,
Mary's motherly heart overstepped the divine plan but, in

doing so, it was an act of love that was divine, and God Who is Love anticipated the hour.

Quietly Mary said to the servants, "Do whatever He tells you."

And Jesus gave His orders. He obeyed His mother—that woman who is all love, and who has many times since done sweet violence to the will of God Himself, hastening His intervention.

Six pots were filled with water—about sixty gallons, as much or more than was needed for the hundreds of invited guests who would attend during the seven days the nuptial feast lasted. Without any ostensible sign, by a mere act of the divine will, that quantity of water was changed into exquisite wine. This was Jesus' first miracle by which He manifested His Messianic power, and on account of it His disciples believed in Him.

Thus, to Mary, is due this first manifestation of His glory and the first adherence of minds to Him. Mother of the poor and mother of faith, she stands in the eyes of all as the mother of the Messiah, the greatest glory ever dreamed of by any Jewish woman.

In that act, her participation in the work of Redemption was once more one of initiative, of deliberate initiative. In reality, she opened the time for the public mission of Christ, as is shown by His answer, stating explicitly that the hour of the God-Man as Savior had not yet come. This was really the greatest miracle, greater than the transubstantiation of a certain quantity of water into wine. The mother had caused that hour to come; she had anticipated it. Some of the ancient exegetes reproached Mary on account of this. She ought to be thanked, for she hastened the Redemption, if only by a few days; and by her intervention—powerful as her intervention has always been—she shortened the exile of the sons of Adam, hastened the preaching of the Gospel, and saved a larger number of souls. She also anticipated in symbol the miracle that changes wine into the Precious Blood of Christ, and makes believers guests at a heavenly banquet.

Besides, she was not unaware of the personal consequences to herself of that anticipation. She was hastening the sword foretold by Simeon, by contradictions, struggles, and the turmoils accompanying the Messianic work. This begun, she would lose her Son, in the sense that He would be entirely given to the glory of God, the salvation of men; freeing Himself from His family according to blood, to give Himself entirely to the family conquered by His Blood. She, the mother, with her gesture of love, was remaining alone, a widow, and hastening the death of that only Son. Once more she is the Co-Redemptrix giving Him up through love.

In a word, for the happiness of two humble creatures, she did not count the sacrifice of her blood. Thus she loved with the heart of her Son. She precipitated the drama of the Redemption for two creatures. She would have done so for only one creature, in the same way as the Word had offered Himself for all men and would be crucified for the only son of one woman.

That episode marks a decisive point in the life of Christ. As it was Mary who gave Him to humanity, so it was Mary who started Him on His public ministry. The thing was done according to God's way, the most humble instruments, in a familiar and simple framework, in the way in which all God's works are commonly presented.

Water changed into wine in the first miracle, wine changed into Blood in the last miracle; and between the first and the last, the Woman of Nazareth stands like the vine from which is generated the fruit that ripens into the life-giving drink. From that moment, the mother of the Holy Family becomes externally the Mother of the human family. The limits of the little home expand into the Church. As the action of Jesus expands, the love of Mary will follow it—or go before it.

The Co-redemptrix

Who could mark, from tears refraining,
Christ's dear mother uncomplaining,
In so great a sorrow bowed? [1]

CHRIST'S PREACHING

As soon as Jesus appeared in the light of His Messianic
Mission, Mary withdraws into its shade. From the miracle in
Cana until His death Jesus will dominate the scene. His hour
has come; it is also Mary's. Their missions are different. Since
the Son will announce the Gospel and prepare minds for the
Redemption, Mary will not throw the shadow of her personality across His path like a jealous mother who wants her
son entirely for herself. Mary knew that the Messiah was for
all men; it was for this that He became incarnate in her
womb. In her consent, she accepted the consequences of that
dependence. With the Son the mother is offered to the service
of humanity.

It is the natural feeling of a normal, reasonable mother
to remain in the background, that the works of her son may
stand out in a full light. When Mary offered herself for the
miracle of the Redemption, she gave herself as the "handmaid
of the Lord" in order that the Lord could give Himself as

---

[1] Quis non posset contristari
Christi Matrem contemplari
Dolentem cum Filio?
STABAT MATER

93

the servant of men. It is exactly this she continues to do: to serve the Son Who is the Lord, she retires in her humility.

Sometimes, she came to Him in the company of other religious women, to render Him the help that only women can give. Most of all, she waited for Him in the little house which she labored to keep open for Him—the Messiah—when He passed through Nazareth, that He might have a place to sleep and a bit of bread to eat.

Her motherly anxiety follows Him in the ups and downs of His divine wanderings, undertaken in order to divinize stubborn, thoughtless men; with an increasing and piercing pain she waited for the end of His Messianic program. She shed many tears over this; tears that would benefit the Evangelization of mankind.

It was martyrdom for her to live so far from Him, and to wait weeks before she had news of Him Whom she loved so much, and still loved—the only flower and fruit of her womb —with the anxious devotion of a mother, a daughter, a spouse. In her was the ardent love of an adoring virgin: the love of one living the life of men with the heart of an archangel.

She knew that by her hidden life, she spared the Divine Evangelizer the pain and sorrow which the sight of her in her heroic renunciation always increased. So Jesus preached, and Mary suffered. Her heart was where His feet trod and on the clump of grass where His head rested. Very often, she had to defend His mission to dense and stupid relatives whose point of view was all for lucrative business. They considered Jesus foolish if His Mission brought in no financial gains. Sometimes the relatives went out to meet the tireless traveler and to remonstrate with Him; to give Him a bit of comon sense, and to explain the wisdom of attending to one's own affairs, thereby earning more money from one's labors. Wouldn't money buy more food and more wine? But Jesus sent them away with certain admonitions which they did not understand and which made most of them angry.

In the teachings of this young "rabbi" there were doctrines that could not please all His kinsfolk, such as "loving strangers," and even "downright enemies." What about vengeance, they wondered. The law of retaliation, the privilege of being the Chosen People? Had He not dared to tell one of His disciples who came asking leave to go first and bury his father "to let the dead bury the dead?"

The worst of it was, He seemed proud of these disturbing theories. One day He declared in public that He had come to bring division—between the son and father, between the daughter and her mother. . . . "What a way of applying the Decalogue," said the relatives. Besides all this, Jesus had stated that a man's enemies were those of his own household; such remarks made the whole tribe blush with shame. As though that was not enough, He had pronounced the beautiful maxim, "He is not worthy of me, that loves father or mother more; he is not worthy of me that loves son or daughter more." [2]

This was, to them, downright impiety! It was an aberration next to blasphemy when He spoke of His own affairs as being "the Kingdom of God," and He presented Himself as the Son of the Most High—he "a nobody." It was sacrilegious! It was madness! So relatives and acquaintances came to the mother, and with voices hoarse from strong drink poured out their convictions at her door. She was His mother; and because of her meekness (which they were sure was due to weakness) she too, was guilty, in allowing such ominous ideas to take root in the mind of this young Man, her Son.

And so Mary was detested because of Him, even by some of her relatives. Although she suffered from this break-down

---

[2] St. Matt. 10:37.

of family unity, which detached her bit by bit from her relatives, she always reacted with gentleness, although they deemed it weakness. She defended the teachings of her nomadic Son with Scriptural reminders, but this only aggravated them the more. "Come with us and hear that stuff!" they exclaimed.

So one day she went with them; they were brimming over with anger and she was overflowing with desire. Only she could love her Son more than herself, more than her own blood, and be worthy of Jesus. It was not hard to find Him, because everywhere one met people who spoke of Him or who had seen Him.

"A brood of vipers, how could you speak to good effect, wicked as you are?" . . . . "a wicked and perverse generation!" [3] These invectives carried by the wind above the heads of the listeners that pressed around Him, reached the ears of the relatives who turned in indignation to the mother and exclaimed, "Do you hear? Do you see? What did we tell you? Is he not mad?"

Jesus was probably speaking from the steps of some small white-washed house to the crowd gathered before Him in the field, so that it was impossible to get near Him. But someone who belonged to that household knew of Mary's arrival and told the Master Who was so concentrated on explaining and forming the Kingdom of God. Someone said to Him, "Here are thy mother and thy brethren standing without, looking for thee." [3]

The Divine Teacher was not disturbed, "He made no answer to the man who brought Him the news," then stretching out His arm towards His disciples with a gesture, He said, "Here are my mother and my brethren! If anyone does the will of my Father who is in heaven, he is my brother and sister, and mother."

---

[3] St. Matt. 12:46–50.

These words must have deeply offended the relatives who had come so far to speak with Him.

"What did I tell you?" said more than one, turning to Mary with revengeful gestures, and perhaps from then on they left her in isolation.

The Gospel does not tell us, but most likely she stayed to listen, or to leave some new garment for Him, or a basket of fruit; and still more likely to be near Him and to embrace Him in a moment of leisure. She understood His words thoroughly, and all their meaning.

Those words were a lesson to some of His uncles and cousins to whom all value consisted in material things, blood, money, vineyards. His words were not in the least any condemnation of family love; those words came from the lips of One Who for love of the Father had come to live among men. His words implied the same as they did when Mary and Joseph found Him in the Temple, and at the time of the miracle in Cana: an affirmation, that spiritual relations are more important than carnal relations, although the latter are not to be denied; and, in both instances, in the Temple and at Cana, Jesus concluded His discourse with a loving submission to His mother. These sudden remarks, blunt with antithesis, must have shocked slow minds.

Another time, when His disciples had invited Him to eat, He had replied, "I have food to eat of which you know nothing." [4] And seeing that they did not understand, He explained, "My meat is to do the will of Him Who sent me." Certainly, He did not mean to repudiate the food that nourished His flesh. In contrasting the spiritual with a blood relationship, Jesus did not intend to reject the latter, least of all His mother, but rather he intended an exaltation of the former, the spiritual. He meant that His disciples (His followers) who believed in Him (Who is Mary's Son) and who

---

[4] St. John 4:32.

later were the Church, were for Him mother and sister and daughter. This meant that she, Mary, His Mother, spouse of the Holy Ghost, and daughter of the Heavenly Father, was on the same level as the Church.

"He who does the will of God is my mother . . ." and she had done the will of His Father, most perfectly. No one on earth had done the will of God with the same completeness and abandonment as she. "Behold the handmaid of the Lord." She was the mother of the Lord Jesus twice over.

The greatness of the Blessed Virgin is not only that she generated the Son of God, but *principally,* as some writers affirm she has done the will of God so perfectly. Hers has been and still remains a maternity of both body and soul.

Always yielding, docile and acquiescent to the Divine Will, she was, according to Jesus' words, not only His mother but also spiritually His sister.

That she should be identified with the Church, although outwardly almost subordinated to it, did not surprise Mary. Her unlimited dignity was equal to the unlimited service to which, with her Son, she had subjected herself. They both were able to stoop to any level in order to be at the service of all, even to the most abject classes of men. Such discussions between the mother and the Son must have been frequent in the little house at Nazareth. To her, therefore, his words were neither new, nor still less offensive.

There were no divergences between her will and the will of Jesus; Her love of the Father found an exact and complete expression in His words; words which she gathered together in her heart for thirty years: not only in her memory but in her heart, where words and gestures blend in the warmth of love. Mary knew her part well. She knew all that Jesus meant when He spoke to those who would make a unity of blood relationship the criterion, which, unless impregnated with the love of God, becomes merely an affirmation of egotism. There must be love, consecration, and sacrifice; a total giving of one's self to men, at the cost of one's own life, and at the sacrificial cost of one's dear ones. This is the revolution of Christ which reaches the sharpest point in service, even to the point of the sword.

But those wordly wise relatives could not understand. Returning to Nazareth, they began to stir up criticism against their morally deteriorated fellow-countrymen, so that when Jesus came His townspeople showed themselves scandalized by Him. It may be that He returned with His mother. The Gospel account gives no lapse in time between the episode just related and His return to Nazareth.

Mary must have suffered much in silence. One reason for that cold reception was due to the remembrance of those relatives that Joseph was only a carpenter, and his widow was there among them. The good resulting from all these great principles was not acceptable when announced, as they were, by One Whose parents were common, ordinary, unimportant people, neither noble nor from the Scribes. Like most people, they too judged the value of God's kingdom in material terms, titles of distinction, and a bank account. If Mary were judged by her clothes, she would not rank higher than a water-carrier. Perhaps the Nazarenes themselves agreed on the proverb that out of Nazareth nothing good could come.

And so, shaking His head sadly, Jesus, Who judged according to the soul's value, answered them—and there was sorrow in His words, "It is only in his own country, in his own home, and among his own kindred, that a prophet goes unhonored." So in the midst of those unbelievers, He performed no miracles, for miracles are flowers that bloom in the furrows of faith.

"I tell you truthfully, everyone who has forsaken home, or brothers, or sisters, or mother, or children, or lands for my sake and for the sake of the gospel, will receive, now in this world, a hundred times their worth, houses, sisters, brothers, mothers, children, and lands, but with persecution; and in the world to come he will receive everlasting life." [5]

So Jesus continued to preach, dictating His rule of Christian heroism. It sounded like madness to the traditionalism of the Jews, classified and divided into tribes, family lineages, as if in fenced-off precincts. Mary understood well. She had made her renunciation for the love of Christ, and so she continued to live in the little town, bearing reproaches, contempt and slander; to suffer her passion for love of Him. So she passed along the narrow streets, bowing beneath the condemnation of her kinsfolk, denunciations from the synagogue and annoyances from the influential. She, the mother of love, the rose of Jericho, the *radix Jesse,* yielded silently to her mission as Mother of Sorrows. She was anticipating the Passion of Christ, her Son.

MARY ON CALVARY

Mary had allowed Jesus to leave her for the glory of His name. She offered Him for His mission as Saviour, releasing Him from family bonds, from duties towards her, His widowed mother, although all this left her alone in a world deaf to her sorrows. The hour was coming when the Father would abandon the Son from Heaven so that love's gift would be complete.

Mary was like the grain of wheat hidden in the earth, which would die and fructify in the Redemption. The handmaid of the Lord continued in silence to die to the world; wrapped in her humility she merited for those who would be redeemed. Nothing more is said of her until the last great hour: the hour of immolation, when her suffering, the work of Jesus, the plan

---

[5] St. Mark 10:29–31.

of the Father in Heaven and the hopes of men on earth, would meet, completed.

For centuries mankind had prepared that altar, the center of gravitation for love and hatred, the point where life meets death. Humanity had need of the gospel of Christ to regain a knowledge of God, it needed the Blood of the Son, to be reconciled with the Father. Humanity was to bury its dead past in Him, and in Him to rebuild a new life.

During most of the period of the Son's public ministry, the mother remained hidden behind His name as good mothers do, and most assuredly, she was the best of mothers. When Jesus was a Child, she was seen; hardly ever was she seen when He was in the fullness of His strength, and during His public life. She came out of her little home only when the hour of suffering struck.

In the liturgical year, when the Church reviews the Gospel scenes and mysteries in the life of Christ, Mary stands out at the beginning and at the end of the cycle; in two decisive moments: at Bethlehem when she gave Christ to life, and in Jerusalem when she gave Him to death. She offered Him in the newness of life that the Old Order might die; she offered Him in death that the New Order might live.

From Galilee she followed her wandering Son in desire and through the information she could gather about Him. He was receiving great acclaim from the crowds for His words and works. When His goodness and wisdom had penetrated their minds, the people spontaneously shouted a blessing that reflected on the mother. "Blessed is the womb that bore thee!" The voice of the people, but it was also the voice of God, repeated the word brought to earth by the archangel.

When the time for the PASCH came—the last one—Mary went up to Jerusalem according to custom, where she was sure to meet Him. Perhaps she was present at the triumph of the palms; hidden in the midst of the crowd she wept tears of joy. Who knows, but that the well-furnished room where our Lord desired to eat the Pasch with His disciples before suffering, was made ready by His mother and the holy women who followed Jesus. Although not present at the Paschal supper with the men, Mary probably saw the Eucharistic celebration in which her Son, after changing bread and wine into His own Body and Blood, gave It to those who sat at table with Him. His Flesh and Blood had first been formed in her and of her, so much so, that it seemed to her she was the offerer, and offering herself. It is understandable how some ecclesiastical writers liken her to both priest and altar.

She must have listened intently to the foretelling of His betrayal; and she suffered with an anguish intensified and made more horrible by the dark night in which Jesus, with His disciples, hid Himself. In that night His bloody immolation was initiated. From that moment Mary became the despised or the pitied mother of a condemned man.

When she heard that He had been taken prisoner, and when later, she saw Him in the courtyard wounded and robed in the red of His own pure Blood, when she listened to the insults and accusations hurled at Him (that seemed to scourge her) all the anguish of her mother love wrapped itself about her heart: a heart supremely sensitive to pain because of the intensity of her love. From that moment she wished only to die with Him. She suffered with Him; every blow of the scourges, every outrage against Him, drenched her soul with blood; faithfully, she bore all the atrocities done to her Son. Her moral martyrdom was, in a sense, a parallel to His physical martyrdom; it was superior to the martyrdom of all the martyrs for Christ because of the perfect love in which she was united to Him. Every suffering of the Son became her own, multiplied seven times over, because falling upon His most pure body, she felt them the more, exquisitely sensitive and pure as she was. In this sense as she suffered with Him, so she was, with Him, the Co-Redeemer.

When Jesus was tortured in the Praetorium, she knew the torture in her own soul as she stood in the square or in the narrow street near by. Her sister, the wife of Cleophas, accompanied her; also Mary Magdalene who had received such great grace from Jesus. And, because she loved Him, this other Mary venerated and followed His mother with loving service. If loving the mother leads to the Son, loving the Son will lead to the mother. The mother of Jesus filled the place of the prisoner in the heart of Magdalene. With the via crucis of Christ, the via crucis of Mary began also, since she walked in His very footprints. A cortège of legionnaires and of servants dragged the condemned One to the place of execution while just behind Him was His Mother with a group of women. Two—the Mother and the Son—were put to death in two different ways.

At the crossroads, or at one of His falls, they met. He was covered with blood and His beautiful features (a copy of her own) were bruised, swollen and almost unrecognizable. The weeping women consoled Him by their courageous fidelity, as the disciples had vanished into thin air through fear.

Then she saw Him being stripped and nailed to the cross. One can imagine how the strokes of the hammer split apart her crucified soul. At the end she had no more tears to shed; she stayed with her eyes burnt by the sun contemplating the terrible scene, dying with her Son Who was dying.

> She stood; He was hanging.
> What He bore on the cross,
> She bore in her heart;
> Interiorly, she too, is a martyr,
> Interiorly, she is entirely consumed
> By the flames of love.

It was then she uttered the groans she had not known at the birth of Jesus. Now she was giving birth to Him in death that the dead might be born again into eternal life. For her part, she was generating Redemption through her Son. Although the essential value is in the Saviour's free giving of His life, the mother freely co-operated also by making the offering of her maternal prerogatives. So, with the Son she was suffering and dying; she too, almost died for the salvation of men and to appease God's justice.

When Jesus offered Himself (and in Him is all the value of His holocaust), His mother had so great a love that she, with Him as Co-Redeemer, could offer Him to the Heavenly Father. In a word, Christ's Sacrifice was hers in a unique way, which she offered in complete union of heart with the Immolated One. Therefore, she has been called since the earliest days of Christianity, "the root," "the generator," "the source of our Sacrifice." Since the Eucharistic miracle embraces the Sacrifice of the Cross, the Ethiopian liturgy exalts Mary, "who is the glory of us all because she brought forth for us, the Eucharist"; and, "on account of her part in her Son's passion" the Church, echoing St. Albert the Great, calls her "a bitter sea"; "a living river of sorrow." When she offered her Son in His Passion, her martyrdom increased in suffering, consequently her love was all bitterness.

Nevertheless, the Evangelists do not record a single word of complaint from her; although she stood so near the cross, she could see His Precious Blood distilled drop by drop from His pure Body. She did not lament, she only suffered. She stood erect, like the priest at the altar. She suffered with the Victim-Priest. She stood, offering Him, the Victim, in the sight of the Jews and of all humanity.

Although she stood at the foot of the cross, she was being immolated on it; she did not die lest she leave Him alone Who seemed to be abandoned, even by His Heavenly Father.

THE DIVINE MATERNITY

Near Mary were the holy women, weeping and trying to console her, while the crowd stared at her, some with pity, others with disdain. They could read in her countenance as she gazed at Jesus (and her presence bore witness to the fact) that she was united with Him to the very end.

John had joined the little group; the disciple whom Jesus loved and who loved Jesus with a richness of love as pure as his virginal youth. On His horrible podium Christ consummated the Sacrifice of His life. At one time His sufferings were so great that He felt Himself utterly forsaken and abandoned by His Father. The cross separated Him from earth; His sacrifice separated Him from Heaven, so that His Blood might freely flow (even if by atrocious means) and fill the gap between Heaven and earth.

It was then, in His last spasms of pain and burning with a fever-thirst, that His Blood poured out, falling upon the scorched ground during the Eve of a Pasch which recalled the sacrificial lamb—the symbol of salvation. He turned His haggard face towards the mob (expressive of scorn and terror) seeing beyond them other men, born and yet to be born, and to each imploring look He gave a drop of His Blood. Then, from His last look at men, for whom He was dying, He turned a lingering one at that little company who loved Him so intensely: His holy Mother, the holy women, and the pure face of St. John.

If, at the Last Supper, His Testament had been one of universal love—the unity of His Church—in this last moment, as His last testament, He gave to the household of believers, a mother.

From the heights of His altar-cross, Jesus said, "Woman, this is thy son." He meant that John, and with John all apos-

tles, disciples and believers—in a word, the Church, were to
be sons of that woman, His mother. And, reciprocally, He said
to John, "This is thy mother."

Jesus was dying, but the motherhood of Mary would go on,
since He was leaving countless descendants as His brothers.
The tragedy of the Passion was being concluded in a great
act of love. Beginning in Bethlehem where Mary gave Jesus
to humanity, it was being completed on Calvary where Jesus
gave Mary to humanity. At the moment when the reconciliation with God the Father was sealed, the divine motherhood
of Mary was fixed forever. Humanity, redeemed by His
Blood, would now take the place of the Immaculate Lamb
before the Father, and in a new relation to the Blessed
Virgin.

She is the woman of sorrows! If her Son was dying on the
cross, another son was born to her beneath the cross—the
Mystical Christ. The Saints all testify: that under the impact
of those drops of life-giving Blood, she suffered the pains of
a mystical birth, through which she would bring forth a
Christian people, thus becoming the Mother of the Church
—the Mystical Body of Christ. What she had accepted in her
Fiat at the Annunciation, was now, on Calvary, confirmed.

After His last gift, in a burning thirst, a tearing of His
flesh, shouts and cries of the mob, and hanging suspended between heaven and earth, the Son of Mary cried out, "It is
achieved!" And bowing His head, He yielded up His spirit.

Mary stood upright; she was like a perpendicular holocaust
between earth and heaven, continuing to suffer. She stayed
until the last outrage, when the stroke of a lance opened and
emptied the heart of the Man-God for the benefit of all men.

Then the sword-thrust, foretold by Simeon, pierced her
heart, to empty over the Dead One in her arms, in Whom is
the compendium of all things and through Whom, humanity,
with all its faults, receives a new purity. It was she who felt
the steel point of the sword. "The mother feels what flesh can

no longer feel; the wound in His side from which water and blood flow like a river to cleanse the world." [6]

> O Mary, most loving mother,
> Wounded by love with the sword
> of the Passion. [7]

This thought, embedded in rhyme by the sorrowing love of medieval poetry, says that in the Blood of Christ (by which men live and still live) were mingled the tears of the mother like a tributary stream of pure water, and His Passion was prolonged in her suffering. Therefore, since she suffered with the Redeemer, she is the Co-Redemptrix.

For a time, the curious mob that looked on saw only her suffering. She was the living pain at the foot of the cross, which was the cause of so much pain. During the terrible darkening of the sun, the rumble of the earthquake that rent the rocks, and amidst the shouts and blasphemies, she—victim with her Son and for her Son—stood facing the world, tortured but fearless. She was crucified with Him, so that her sorrowing love and the offering of herself, fused in His oblation, might be absolute. This is the whole Sacrifice. Here begins the continuous Sacrifice of the Mass in which the human family re-lives Christ on the Cross, with the mother at the foot of the cross surrounded by both executioners and disciples; here tears and love are always united, love that no lance can destroy and hatred that dashes itself against that gibbet.

---

[6] A.H. 43, 83. "In compassione B.V.M."
[7] *Ibid.,* 34,14.

Mother
of the Church

Mother of Justification, and of the justified,
Mother of Reconciliation, and of the reconciled;
Mother of Salvation, and of the saved,
Mother of the Saviour, and our Mother.

ST. ANSELM

THE PIETÀ

People who had looked on at the Crucifixion as at a free show, now dispersed through the outskirts of Jerusalem—the city of sacrifices and the slayer of prophets—and scattered to their houses. They commented on what had happened with knowing looks; most of them were satisfied with the punishment meted out to the two thieves, and even more so to that impostor in the center Who had claimed to be the Son of God and then was unable to free Himself from the gibbet. They were more satisfied because that type of peaceful Messiah in no way corresponded with the expectations of the multitude. They hoped for a conquering hero, one capable of routing the bands of Romans and avenging the people of God who were now subjected to those idolaters.

The soldiers and the women, together with John and Mary, remained at the top of the mount. The soldiers removed the nails, loosened the bodies, took down the bar of the cross, and left; dragging the tools, chains and garments of the crucified after them. They set out for the barracks or for an inn, for they were thirsty.

Since the bodies were loosened from the nails, they were

108

left to relatives. Neither political nor religious authorities, fear nor hatred could use them any longer. Let their intimate relatives have them.

Taking down the Body of Jesus from the cross has been recalled by numerous paintings in Christian art: an expression of Christian piety. The mother took her Son in her arms as when she brought Him forth. Bent and exhausted, she held Him in a loving embrace. In Siena there is a "Taking Down From the Cross" by Duccio. His hands detached from the nails, the bloodless body of Jesus weighs down upon the face and on the shoulder of the Mother as if He were a boy heavy with sleep. She receives Him with tears and caresses, her eyes drinking in the sight of that face so spotted with blood. Once more she is the sole arbitrator of that adorable Body.

When He was placed on the ground she covered Him with her veil and with her kisses. Christ's stiffened and discolored body looked like the body of a child numb and blue with cold asking for help from his mother. She raised Him to her knees and cradled Him, as when a child, He had gone to sleep on her lap. Tearfully she murmured, "My Son! My Son!" It was as if she wished to send His Blood, now poured out on the hard earth and impregnating It with His divinity, coursing again through His veins.

For a long time she remained motionless, in a posture that made her the mother of a dead man—Mother of the first Martyr. Would she not be the mother of numberless martyrs, who would be tortured, mutilated, bled, sawed in pieces, drowned or put to death from the same old calumnies and with the same savage instruments, for preaching and confessing Him? Mary, mother of the living, shed then the first tears of anguish over the dead; all who were offered to God in order that others might live. It seemed to her then that she was once more carrying the Christ-Child, as if a new life was beginning and joined with the end.

9. *Nazareth*

MOTHER OF THE RISEN CHRIST

Mary Magdalene and the other women were weeping although trying to speak words of comfort to Mary of Nazareth. With loving insistence they tried to take her away. When Joseph of Arimathea came to carry the body away and bury it in his own tomb newly hewn in a rock, Mary and John accompanied her Son to the grave. The tearful band started in haste, for evening was nigh and it was the eve of the Pasch, the sabbath was about to begin. Jesus had finished His suffering and was on His way to rest; the mother continued to die.

The body was washed, wrapped in a linen sheet and laid in a hollow place inside the rock. Mary lingered, drinking in with her eyes that lifeless face and looking for the last bit of radiance emanating from under those closed eyelids. When the huge stone was rolled to the entrance she clung to it, calling Him again and again by name until, prostrated with grief, John took her to his hospitable home. There she continued to mourn, while her Son, having descended into the kingdom of death, was awakening life with strokes of radiant glory.

The following day was the great Sabbath and the people kept holiday. During the general suspension of all activity in Jerusalem, Mary remained at home, keeping her sorrowful watch, praying to God and to her Son. Early the following morning, the women, her friends, went to the place of sepulchre, and found with fear and amazement, that the stone was rolled back from the entrance and the body taken away.

Trembling, they were stopping to examine the slab upon which the body had been laid when two angels emerged from the tomb and said to them, "Why are you seeking one who is alive, here among the dead? He is not here, He has risen again." The tomb held no more interest for them. They scattered in haste, carried away with joy over His resurrection and this confirmation of His own prophecies. Running to the Apostles, they told them the news. It was the women, Mary's companions, who were the apostles of the resurrection to the Apostles themselves. What a reward for their humble fidelity!

In all probability, Mary, too, had left the city, going towards the garden of Joseph of Arimathea and the tomb of Jesus. Perhaps, within the garden enclosure, her Son came to meet her, as radiant as if He had descended from the sun. Her Son was now gloriously re-united to the Father. She gave full rein to her joy, and adored Him as God. Thus He repaid her with a unique happiness for all she had suffered in her long, faithful, and active participation in the miracle, now accomplished.

The Gospel makes no mention of this meeting; perhaps, Mary did not reveal it to her companions or to John. It had been so dazzling, so intimate and so tremendous. It was all for herself; one of those experiences one hesitates to disclose and knows not how to describe. An ancient tradition holds as most probable that the first appearance of the Risen Christ was to His mother—the one who had the greatest right to see Him.[1]

Now that the Reconciliation was accomplished and the God-Man had given His life as a pledge of the new Re-union between divinity and humanity (God's harmonious sharing with believers on earth), the unfolding of the Redemption moved rapidly. The divine and human activity in the Church was initiated when Jesus ascended into Heaven. His visible presence was replaced by the visible Church; and His works of evangelization were continued by the Apostles. Although

---

[1] In the Spiritual Exercises of St. Ignatius, he says, "Jesus appeared to the Virgin Mary; and although this is not mentioned in Scripture, still it is considered as mentioned when it says that He appeared to many others, for the Scripture supposes us to have understanding, according as it is written, 'Are ye also without understanding?'" p. 101.

Mary's heart was ever turned towards her Son in glory, she continued to be for the Apostles and disciples what she had been to Jesus Himself; in them, the Church, her Son remained visible. The Church became her Child, being the Mystical Body of her Son Himself. In the same manner as she had watched over the growth of the Child-Jesus, so she guided the development and growth of the Church to which she gladly gave her care, her counsels, and her advice.

Her life was lived from now on in union with the nascent Church, as she had been and united with her Boy-Christ. She belongs to the Church and the Church belongs to her. In both, Christ Jesus lives and radiates His Spirit. In serving the Church, which is from God, Mary continues her vocation as "handmaid of the Lord."

Common life for the little group in the Cenacle was, above all else, prayer. They prepared for their future activity by uniting their souls with Jesus, so that He might reign there in each and in all in the plenitude of His Spirit, and that all their works might be entirely His. They were all of one mind; they grew daily in wisdom, as the Christ Child had done under the guidance of Mary. She in their midst was a visible witness to Him that strengthened their fidelity to Him as their Saviour.

She was also an authority in all they had been taught by her own teaching, telling them all she had heard from the lips of Jesus during those intimate years spent at Nazareth; unveiling the sweetest mysteries of the Redemption. The Apostles listened, and the Evangelists gathered up, from her oral accounts, memories, and testimonies, what they have related in their writings for the benefit of distant brethren of the faith.

In the meantime, souls gathered about her in prayer were uplifted; from her thoughts their minds were growing stronger in knowledge and in faith; near her, they experienced a pure joy that comes from personal contact with the supernatural, a joy which was due, in large part, although hidden, to her virginal motherhood.

RETURN OF THE SPOUSE

The infant Community stands as the model of the Church for all times. It is made up of a hierarchy, in an ascending order: disciples (or believers); above them, the Apostles; then Mary with her extraordinary graces, while above all is the Blessed Trinity. Jesus had not left His followers orphans. He had organized them into a Mystical Body, drawing life from His Precious Blood, united to Him in an inseparable manner, and last of all, He had given them His mother to be their Mother. That was the Church. Christ is the Head; the disciples are the members under the authority of Peter and the Apostles; Mary is the Mother. Thus composed organically, the life of Christ in His Church continues. In place of Judas another Apostle was chosen; and this election was an act of Divine choice. What had been done personally by Christ was now done under the eye of Mary and with the assistance of Mary. For the Church could not exist without Jesus, nor without Mary. God was the Father: Mary, the Mother.

Christian conscience, enlightened by revelation, had seen very early the mystical identity of the Church, with Christ as Head, and the striking analogy of the Church to Mary: each one a virgin and a mother; both endowed with perpetual virginity and a holy fecundity. And, as in the Church, faith grows and expands, so also, love for Mary continues to grow and increase.

On the day of Pentecost, the Holy Ghost in flames of fire invaded the Cenacle where the Saints were gathered about Mary. It was an investiture. The Holy Ghost took possession of all there. The Blessed Virgin remembered that other investiture of her Conception where was begun the union of the Eternal Word with human nature, and this union was now culminating in the creation of the Church. Pentecost was for Mary another visible meeting with her Spouse, the Holy Spirit. Grace and vigor penetrated the persons of those present in the Cenacle, transfiguring them. For Mary the cycle was now concluded; the cycle of the visible manifestation of the Holy Spirit, of her witnessing before men and by her physical participation. She had brought the Holy Spirit to the Church; better still, in identifying her with the Church, He made known to men those eternal espousals that gave to men Jesus in Bethlehem and give Him now and for all eternity.

Her place was henceforth in the bosom of Eternal Love, to receive there for herself a reward, a new dignity beyond all thought and a power to continue her maternal jurisdiction through Jesus in His Church.

Mary lived with the Church when it was in its infancy. In feeding her Child at the breast, had she not fed the Church? Now invested with the gifts of the Holy Spirit (gifts, because since they belong to the Spouse they belong also to the Bride—Mary), the Church will come of age: expanding beyond the small racial limits of the Hebrew people, to all people. The Church will take on the divine attribute of immortality and the power of infallibility in its activity throughout the world.

The first Apostles soon added to their followers many energetic ones like St. Paul who undertook to convert the peoples of Europe and Asia. Even in Rome the name of Jesus was being invoked.

Mary assisted her Son's Apostles and visited some of the centers where more intense evangelization had been done. She had probably been to Ephesus with St. John, where St. Paul had opened a door wide for the Gospel, and from there word came to her of the first martyrs. The Church was advancing with gigantic steps; it was fighting and dying, and in dying giving new life to the world. Now she could leave it. The Apostles had had the joy of her presence as long as was necessary for them. They now understood that the Church resembled Mary and that she was the prototype of the Church. Both Mary and the Church are virgin-mothers; both are Spouses of the Holy Ghost.

THE ASSUMPTION

The day came when the Apostles would have to take care of themselves. From the abyss of Eternity, God the Father assisted them; Jesus the Son fed them; the Holy Ghost enlightened them; so the Virgin Mother, to whom, in a way, was entrusted the dominion and distribution of the treasures of the Trinity, could now leave the Apostles, as far as her physical presence was concerned. Heavy with merits rather than with years, she yielded to the desire of God the Son, of the Holy Ghost her Spouse, of the Heavenly Father, and was drawn to the Trinity Whose instrument she had been in the regeneration of humanity. The Blessed Trinity longed for her, and she longed to be with Them.

The day came when she serenely and sweetly slept away in the presence of the Apostles, as peaceful and innocent of death as all human creatures would have been had it not been for the fall of Eve, the first mother. Drawn by her ardent desire to be united with the Trinity, Mary passed to Heaven in a kind of ecstasy, in an effusion of love just as the Son of her love had expired on the terrible cross. It has also been said that she died of the invisible wound received on Calvary when her Son was crucified.

Death for her was not such as we know and suffer; it was something sweet and swift. The theologians describe her death in various terms: a brief pause, a quiet passing, a quick transit, a sleep, a death that was a coming into life. Her death was a counterpart of the virginal birth that was accomplished without pain.

A choir of angels invaded the small room. From the midst of the Apostles and the angels, Jesus took the soul of His most sweet Mother—the All-Pure, the all-holy, the all-fair—and with exulting joy carried it to Heaven.

From the earliest centuries Christian art has depicted this scene of the Assumption of Mary as a going forth of the soul of a maiden out of her sleeping body into the hands of the Redeemer. It was the Mother's return to the Son, like a birth into the Eternal Life of the Son. In fact, Mary was *born* into the celestial courts of Paradise.

Her birth into Heaven was a day of such joy as the human mind cannot conceive. It was a kind of inebriation of the Holy Spirit overflowing on all the angelic hosts and upon the souls of the blessed. It was a day of jubilation in which the hopes of all times broke forth into the fullness of heavenly bliss.

The angels and Saints had a Mother. They had been waiting for her forever. From the moment she entered, the heavenly courts were filled with a new peace and lighted with a new light, that of Virginal Motherhood. It was not that aught was missing in the joy of the blessed, rather, God added something: the smile of Mary, who, being the masterpiece of the Trinity, gathers together the joyous adoration of the angels and Saints in an effusion of love towards the Blessed Trinity. But the greater jubilation was that of God the Son, Who once clothed in flesh, had a double yearning for her presence. The reparation to the Father and the victory of the Son's Love had been made possible through her.

The Mother is reunited to her Son in the Eternal kingdom of God, beyond the realm of passion and death. As her humility had been the greatest on earth, so now her glory is greatest in Heaven. Hers is an incomparable triumph.

The marvelous mystery of God humbling Himself to take on the flesh of Mary, is now reversed in the mystery of Mary raised up as Queen of Heaven through the gratitude of her Son. This glory was complete when her stainless body was reunited to her pure soul. As the Son had resumed His Body before the decay of the grave had touched it, so likewise the body of Mary, which had been placed in a tomb, probably in Jerusalem, was at once reunited to her immortal soul. According to tradition, when the Apostle Thomas, who had not been present to witness the falling asleep of that most sweet Mother, returned to venerate her body, he found the tomb empty.

Then, in Mary's stainless flesh and blood, humanity entered into the home of pure spirits, and definitely sealed the union between the Heavenly Father and His children. Our resurrection from the dead was guaranteed anew, and the fullness of grace flowing from the wonderful dignity of the Mother of God was now revealed.

The flesh that had given Incarnate Life to the Saviour should not suffer corruption. Her dignity as Mother of God would not square with that, for her flesh, free from all stain was not subject to the law of the grave. And so she was rejoined to the Body of her Son, for the "flesh of Christ is the flesh of Mary."

The stem is rejoined to the flower, the womb to its fruit. Her virginal body was not destined to be touched by the process of decay but rather, because having suffered in union with Christ, she was destined to be immediately raised to glory with Christ. Finally, it was not fitting that her body should suffer the loss of integrity. She, who generated the vivifying Head of the Church, should participate in the incorruptible and imperishable vitality of that immortal organism. The Assumption of the Blessed Virgin Mary is not yet an official dogma of the Church; perhaps not so much that it is doubted, but because it is not doubted and so universally accepted.

It is a fact imbedded in the mind of the Church. No other feast, except perhaps Christmas, is so universally popular, so jubilantly celebrated as the Assumption, Mary's birthday into glory.

Down the centuries, in mid-August of every year, Church belfries awaken like so many children on holiday, and pour down their rejoicing peals upon the house-tops and country-side. On the warm evening of the Vigil, all the little villages, brightly lighted, shine like so many clusters of stars, and amidst the flashing of fireworks and general rejoicing, the endless, loving lists of Mary's titles (an unsuccessful attempt to exhaust the praises of the Most-Pure) are sung. The infinite gladness of her return to her Son is the cause in every home of family joy. It stirs the little ones and moves the old folk to tears. Every home is consciously keeping holiday for a deeper reason; every house is a tiny Church on earth and re-news, in a tiny way, the exultation of the great Church Triumphant.

Popular piety? Here is the saying true, Vox POPULI, Vox DEI. Faith expresses itself in graceful, plastic figures. These statues are seen in many public squares and on the threshing floors,[2] representing the meeting of the Son with the Mother in Heaven in a glorious reunion. A multitude of Saints, patrons of the Arts and Guilds, are carried in procession.

All is joy, recalling the happiness of Christmas, and ex-pressing the joy of the Church in the *transitus* of Mary; also the Church's joy for her own *transitus* with Mary. "How beautiful and splendid to behold," exclaims St. John Dama-scene. "Thou art the flower of the field, the lily amid thorns; Thou makest death to smile." [3]

---

[2] The threshing floor is often used as the dancing place of the village.
[3] P.G. 96,728–716,7.

If this glorious Assumption of Mary into Heaven is not recorded in the New Testament writings, it was probably deemed unwise to put before people, so recently converted from paganism and Judaism, the unique privilege of Mary as a temple of God. It could have been misunderstood—as, indeed it was, even by the Christians not fully permeated with Christ—to regard her as the deity in a temple. But in their private conversations, the Apostles and their disciples spoke of it, as one would about news from their heavenly home and in telling of the joys of that home.

Thus the doctrine regarding the Assumption of the Blessed Virgin Mary has been handed down from father to son, like other treasured family possessions; it is the transmission of a treasure running through all generations like a river of grace. Some references to the fact found expression in the Apocryphal writings. On account of their antiquity, these witness to the deep root the doctrine has taken in the consciousness of Christians. As soon as they could, the faithful gave expression to their belief in marbles and colors, so that the Mother and Son, united in glory, were visibly seen and associated in their devotions of love.

Mary of Nazareth is now taken up into glory where, vibrant with life and grace—the heart of the Church Triumphant—she stands as the guarantee for the final assembly of all the faithful in the spirit and in the flesh. She is the heart and queen, because to serve God is to reign. No creature has ever so completely become the servant of the Most High God as she; and no mortal has ever been raised to a power and glory such as hers.

And now the Son "in the center of the rotating white rose" [4] with the Saints, amidst the hosannas and hymns of triumph, crowns her as Queen. She too, with her Son and by her Son, has overcome the world, and she is Mother of the

---

[4] Dante's Paradiso, Canto 31.

Church Militant. In Heaven she celebrates the royal victory
of the Christian militia. The three parts of the Church, which
had in Jesus a King, now have in Mary a Queen to bring them
a superabundance of joy and hope and help.

St. Gertrude, divinely enlightened, declares that Mary is
the most powerful after the Father, has the most wisdom after
the Son, and loves most after the Holy Ghost. She is the joy
and delight of the Blessed Trinity. The three Divine Persons
have in her a Daughter, a Spouse and a Mother; and under
these three titles love her with an infinite love.

Union with God which had always been hers, was now completed by a triple bond: so that the power of the Father was
communicated to Mary, the daughter; the Wisdom of the Son
given to the Mother; and the sanctifying gifts of the Holy
Spirit are also the gifts of Mary, the Spouse, because the
Bridegroom and the Bride are one.

This fact of intimately associating a woman to the divine
attributes of God, corresponds with the fact that she had associated humanity to God. On this account, she is called
Mediatrix because she distributes to men the graces of the
Trinity with hands that had carried God the Son, just as she
had given men Jesus, the Redeemer. In a word, she continues
to act as a Mother.[5]

---

[5] "Only until the end of time will the Blessed Virgin be tranquil; as long as
the world lasts, she—the Mother of a multitude—will be busy running from
one to another."

CURÉ D'ARS, "Petite Fleurs," XI.

The Gate and
Window of Heaven

O Virgin! O Lady! All Holy!
What names of beauty all languages
  keep for thee!
More than one nation is proud of thee,
And boasts of thy gentle guardianship.
          —MANZONI: *Il nome di Maria*

THE ACTION OF MARY AS QUEEN

In God's Divine plan of life, to be invisible does not mean
that souls cease to be beneficently active. At the very moment
when Jesus ascended into Heaven, withdrawing His physical
presence from His Apostles, He commanded them to go out
and evangelize the whole world. Thus, it was after He had
gone that the Church took His place everywhere. When the
Church has embraced the full number of redeemed souls, she
will be the *Christus totus;* until then, she continues to build
up Christ in the world.

This is true also of the Mother. When she was withdrawn
from our sight, her Motherhood was elevated and, because
elevated, it was widened, lifted up to God, her Motherhood
became universal. Where Jesus reaches, she reaches. Now that
she has entered into glory, her control and distribution of
grace envelops the Church. The chronicles of her life are
filled with the signs of her continual intervention.

To know her has made innumerable lovers of her. Her
biography is interwoven with the existence of religious orders

121

and of baptized nations. The story of her life is embroidered
with poetry, and weaves a strand of virginal beauty into the
warp and woof of the world's history. The more Christianity
has entered into the heart of humanity, the more has the
glorious Virgin Mary penetrated its spirituality, art, literature
and political economy. Just as men attempted to hate that
fount of love during her earthly life, so now they attempt to
deny that source of abundant grace, considering it all as a
small matter originating in a handful of apocryphal writings.

In the meantime, millions of Christian souls live by this
love and knowledge of our Blessed Mother; hundreds of spiritual and corporal good works spring from her; the miraculous fountains of grace and healing break forth from her;
enamored poems and books are inspired by her. Her history
can be summed up in two phases: first, a shower of graces,
compared to the light cloud seen by the prophets coming so
quickly with its burden of refreshing rain; and secondly, the
daily and increasing love ever mounting to her from her
children. They yearn to make their love of her person an en-
during one, something very characteristic of the relations of
men with this woman.

Such love for Mary is not surprising; it is the sublimation
of the faculty for loving given to human beings, and it is a
measure of the love with which God loves the Virgin from all
eternity. In order to choose her as Daughter, Mother and
Spouse, the uncreated Trinity must have loved her better
than any one created person, and more than all other creatures. Our love for her is but a pale shadow compared to the
love of the Blessed Trinity.

God loved her more than any creature. . . . Her greatness
marks the knitting together of humanity with divinity; it
marks the horizon where heaven and earth meet and give the
kiss of reconciliation. Petty, jealous sons have resented her
greatness; and yet it is quite in the right order of things that

the greatness of the Son should reflect on the Mother. What is the greatness of Mary? It consists in this: she is the mother of Jesus; therefore, the Mother of God. Hers is the most unique dignity on account of which he is most unique among creatures. "She has no equal—before nor after." [1]

The fear that love for Mary might lessen love for Christ comes from shortsightedness, since she was first loved by the Blessed Trinity. The greatness of the Blessed Virgin is perceived by men in proportion as they come nearer to God. It was the Saints who discovered her, because sanctity is the soul's approach to God, aided by a divine light directed on the intelligence. Thus, the nearer one comes to God the clearer Mary is seen. We can say that Mary is discovered in God.

Our sonship in God could not be complete if it lacked a mother; without Mary we would be motherless, even if we had the Fatherhood of God. This Fatherhood we have found only because Mary made herself our Mother. Here lies the mystery of her greatness, and this is the reason endless lines of her children kneel at her feet; here is the mystery of divine life and the criterion for human life.

Considering her great dignity and the power that flows from her, our love for Mary becomes extraordinary veneration, which is called hyperdulia, but it takes nothing from the adoration due to God, for in her we venerate the greatest work of the Trinity. An artist is not depreciated when his masterpiece is praised; the Son suffers no displeasure if we praise her who bore Him.

In listing and explaining the forty special reasons for which the redeemed owe continuous and uninterrupted service and praise to the Virgin, St. Albert the Great reminds us that, through her, in her and from her, glory to the Father, the Son, and the Holy Spirit has been increased; and that

---

[1] Liturgy.

through her, in her, with her and from her, the world has had, has, and will have the whole of good, which is Christ; for, having found Mary, it has found all good." [2] Although exalted in glory, Mary has not lost the characteristics of her nature. She is the same to us as she is to the Apostles, only with glory added.

She remains for us the Woman, intelligent and ready, as appears from her replies to the Archangel and to Elizabeth. Whole nations have experienced her prophetic intuitions that reveal the hidden desires in the hearts of those who invoke her. All her life she was humble and prudent; she awakens in us the need of silence, such as hers was in Nazareth, that we may act with wisdom, as she did in Cana. She was learned and knew the Scriptures: at once she understood the angel's speech. She was obedient and generous in faith; therefore known as the seat of Wisdom of Him Whose mother she is. Whoever yields to her inspirations has found a sure way in the mysteries of God.

She is remembered for her deep spirituality. We met her first as a maiden, praying as she worked; and in order to offer adoration to God her Father, she went on long hard pilgrimages to Jerusalem. She continues to lead souls to her Son because this is her mission: to conquer the love of creatures for their Creator. It is a mission of maternal grace, a prolongation of her natural motherhood.

Mary reveals herself as the strong Woman. This she proves by the Magnificat, in facing the terrors of Herod's persecution, the sorrows of her widowhood and the tortures of the Crucifixion. Therefore, if our veneration and love for her is sincere and honest, we will not give way to faint-heartedness, morbidness and moral weakness in the face of trouble.

She is often compared to an army in battle array; depicted crushing the head of the serpent, undoing the fall of Eve,

---

[2] "De Laudibus Mariae Virginis," lib. II,1.

Mary

Most Holy

in the

New

Testament

THE ESPOUSALS — *A. Panigati*

... And Jacob begot Joseph, the husband of Mary, and of her was born Jesus who is called Christ.   MATTHEW 1

THE ANNUNCIATION — *A. Panigati*
The Angel said to Mary, "The Holy Spirit shall come upon thee, and
the power of the Most High shall overshadow thee; and therefore the
Holy One to be born shall be called the Son of God."   LUKE 1

THE NATIVITY — *A. Panigati*
It came to pass that the days for her to be delivered were fulfilled, and Mary brought forth her firstborn son, and wrapped him in swaddling clothes and laid him in a manger, because there was no room for them in the inn. LUKE 2

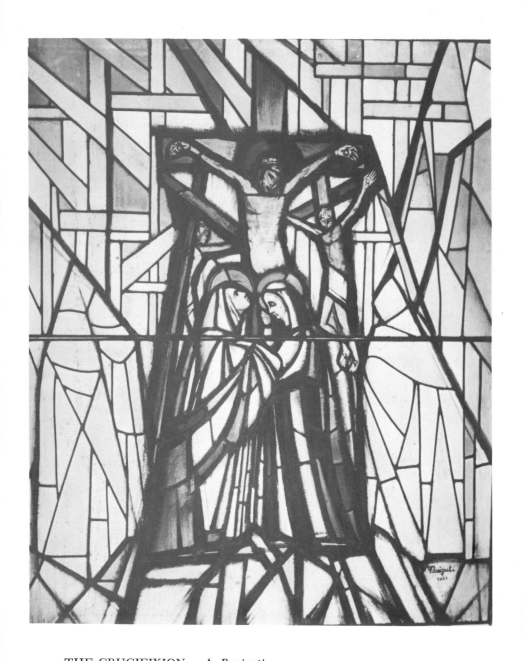

THE CRUCIFIXION — A. *Panigati*
There were standing by the cross of Jesus His mother, and His mother's
sister Mary of Cleophas and Mary Magdalene.   JOHN 19

CORONATION OF THE BLESSED VIRGIN MARY — *A. Panigati*
Most worthy Queen of the world, ever Virgin Mary, intercede for our
peace and salvation, you who gave birth to Christ our Lord, Savior
of all.   LITURGY, FEAST OF QUEENSHIP OF MARY

and at every turn her intervention among men is stamped with strength. The truth is, that the few episodes about her in the Gospels, and the innumerable favors granted by her in glory, prove that she is endowed with all gifts. She is *full of grace,* the reservoir of sanctity, the Masterpiece of the Trinity.

Some of her special characteristics strike us more today—her Motherhood; her mediating power (as seen at Cana); the Woman concerned with the needs of others and inducing her Son to act in their behalf; her humility and purity flowering over the universe. St. Gertrude used to invoke her as "the most pure lily of the glorious and ever-peaceful Trinity."

THE TITLES OF MARY

It is an unending effort to define Mary—a magnificent and thrilling effort, because in coming near to her every man becomes a poet; and out of the enchantment of his imaginations there buds forth fairylike epithets and glowing imagery. In the East, the Fathers of the first centuries called her the all-holy, the Temple of God, Heaven, the spotless lily, dove without blemish, the innocent one, the pure turtle dove, the lamp that is never extinguished, the bearer and mother of light, glory of the Church, the undefiled one, mother of sanctity, most pure source of the water of life, the throne of God, an incorruptible flower, plant of incorruption, the paradise of immortality, Spouse of the Trinity, the unique bridge between God and men, ladder reaching to Heaven, gate of Paradise, new Mother and bosom of regeneration, union and peace between God and men. . . .

"What an abyss of miracles," exclaims St. John Damascene. "She is the fountain of healing for the whole world, the apex of sanctity, the city of God watered by the waves of divine love; she is all fair, most near to God, dispenser of riches, with the plenitude of glory. To those who struggle in life,

10. *Nazareth*

Mary is rest and to the afflicted she is consolation. To the shipwrecked, she is a port of safety, pardon for sinners, comfort of the oppressed, refuge of all who call upon her. She is the great honor of creation."

Her titles listed in the Litany of Loretto had been accumulated already in the Oriental invocations. They have been gathered in lists of fifties and of hundreds. St. John Damascene had used them all except "morning star." This exquisite epithet shines early on the poetical horizon of the western hemisphere. "Hail, star of the sea," sang the early Christians in the west, as the fury of persecution from without and the impact of passions from within made them think of the tempestuous ocean.

Thus, St. Bernard, contemplating the Blessed Virgin, spontaneously wrote these verses in a prose like a corymb flower in the center of verdant foliage:

> If the hurricane of temptation rises against thee,
> Or thou art running upon the rocks of trouble,
> Look to the star, call upon Mary.
> In danger, difficulty, or doubt,
> Think of Mary, call upon Mary.
> Let her never be away from thy heart,
>   or from thy lips.[3]

St. Albert of Cologne with keen insight lifted his head from his well-thumbed parchments and wrote:

> Star of the East,
> Never failing splendor
> And noble light;
> Sun thou art, that knows
>   no eclipse,

---

[3] St. Bernard, Hom. 3, super Missus.

> The moon that begets the sun,
> Always beloved.[4]

It was night everywhere in the world, and Mary was beckoning to her children, twinkling her pure light so that, East and West, although divided on other points, were united on this one, and vied with each other in exalting the Mother of God. This alone is sufficient proof of their supernatural brotherhood, as it is a proof that the Mother is *"Mater unitatis,"* the Mother who unifies: the Mother of unity.

Many of the titles found in the East recur in the writings of the Latin Fathers. Mary is described as the royal palace of the Eternal King, the hall of heavenly sacraments, a door ever closed; the eastern door of the sanctuary, virginal lily, virgin soil, and many others.

Saint Ambrose, Prudentius, Sedulius, Venantius Fortunatus jewel their poetry with gracious and pleasing titles that describe the excellence of her virginal motherhood. Fulbert of Chartres calls her the *"Forma Dei,"*—the Form of God. Thus the imagination has flowered and developed with the spreading of the Gospel over a broken Europe and down the march of time. Nor do they exhaust her titles, rather they add to them. She is called the lily of purity, the paradise of sanctity, our only hope after Christ, Queen of clemency, and olive of mercy. St. Gertrude calls herself "Mary's little sister"; and calls Mary the model of modesty and chastity, the star of prophecy, and the way of life.

Others have proclaimed her the ruler of heaven and vase of divinity, gate of the prince, diadem of the king, bridge for sinners, fountain of running water in Paradise, rule of sanc-

---

[4] A.H. 42, 94 O Lucifer oriens, Splendor indeficiens,
        Lux prae clara.
        Sol eclipsim nesciens, luna sola pariens,
        Semper cara.

tity, hope of the desperate, gem of chastity, flower of dignity, queen of flowers, honor of virgins, virginal temple of God, rose of spring—and this particular invocation, *"Rosa vernans,"* characterizes the praise of all times. Mary is called the source of dogma, house of perfumes, true glossary of the Scriptures, vine of Engaddi, starry window, and restorer of justice. Then, at last, they all sigh and say simply, *"Mater Dei, Mater mei!"* "Mother of God and my Mother!" with sweet abandonment to her.

They salute her, "Hail, our life and sure way." There are many hymns in the Middle Ages on the "names and titles of the Blessed Virgin Mary," one of them has twenty-seven verses of eight lines each, and in each verse there are seven titles. Another hymn has three hundred and seventy-five verses and as many titles. All the beautiful and charming things that can be said of her in human language have been said. She is the completeness of beauty.

How Love for Mary Expands

In all truth the name of Mary is poetry. As the Apostles made known the name of Jesus in the public squares and in homes, they also left the name of Mary in the hearts of men. Under the shadow of love for the Son there blossomed love for the Mother. Very soon love for her spread beyond the confines of Palestine and began to put out shoots as a chaste flower, exhaling the sweet odor of a new womanhood, in a world darkened by feminine deities of lust and cruelty.

Mary's deeds of charity, beauty and poetry adorn the paths of men with gems, and garland them with fragrance during their brief sojourn on earth. She brought loving kindness to a world ruled by the gods of war, and she softens hard, stony hearts.

At first the faithful did not often utter her name, which

glowed softly like a pearl, but kept it hidden in their hearts with their love lest it be tarnished by contact with idolatry. Thus sheltered within the intimacy of their affections, it was kept pure. Love for Mary and her name took deep root in the souls of the early Christians. Meanwhile, as prayer and knowledge of Christian dogmas followed upon the overthrow of Mosaism and pagan rationalism, the place and function of the Co-Redemptrix grew steadily clearer in the Christian conscience.

Mary is not mentioned by St. Paul in his Epistles; the name of Christ is always there; but St. Paul's writings are polemical, and he is concerned only in making Christ known and understood. No one would introduce the name of Mary without a reason, because in one's loving attraction for a woman, not only her person but also her name is shielded. However, in St. Luke's Gospel, he speaks of her with lyric love, and St. Luke was spurred on to write and guided by St. Paul.

St. Paul was a traveler and a fighter for Christ. It may have been either in Jerusalem or in Ephesus that he received, directly from the Blessed Virgin, those confidences that make the third Gospel so precious to us. St. John, who wrote his profound revelations at Patmos, had acquired from his intimate associations with Mary, and from her teachings his knowledge of those deep, celestial mysteries, which she guarded.

At Patmos, St. John saw her in glory again: the WOMAN, clothed with the sun, a crown of twelve stars around her head, the moon beneath her feet for a footstool and, because she was the Mother of the Lord, she stood as Queen of the world. The serpent, risen up against the Child born of her was now defeated, spewing forth his anger against her—the WOMAN who was the first one victorious over him. In his rage, he continues to wage war on those born of her, that is, Christians;

because they are her children and keep the commandments of the Lord.

Mary's sweet womanliness gave strength and light to the Apostles; and they loved her too well to expose her name without necessity to the malicious diatribes of ambitious men. As soon as Christian communities were formed, her name emerged from silence like moonlight appearing through the parting clouds. At first she was called the Virgin of virgins; after her glorious assumption into Heaven, she was Mother of God; then successively, Advocate of Sinners, and the Immaculate Conception.

St. Ignatius of Antioch, a disciple of St. John, speaks of her, and in doing so, uses the word "received:" that is, he received this knowledge from St. John himself and from the Church which, in the beginning, was formed around Mary, born from her bosom.

Among Christians, well grounded in the faith, there was never any fear that the mention of this WOMAN so enriched with divine attributes, might induce those converted from paganism to worship her, mistaking her for some goddess out of the polytheistic cults about them. In fact, in the course of time, the list of Mary's attributes began to be known, just as were those of Christ, when heretics and protestants began to make their assault on both. It was heresy that provoked dogmatic definitions by the Church; it was the threatening danger of seeing the distinctive traits of the Blessed Virgin tarnished that induced the Church to define them so clearly.

St. Ignatius of Antioch had already substantiated the Incarnation by asserting that Jesus was from Mary and from God; one the mother and the other the Father. Soon the virginity of the mother was recognized as a stupendous proof of the divinity of the Son. St. Justin Martyr emphasizes the antithesis between Mary and Eve. A little later at Rome, Hippolitus uses the title THEOTOKOS, that is, "Mother of

God." Over this title battle raged, until the Council of Ephesus definitely defined the Motherhood of the Virgin.

THEOTOKOS, Mother of God, is invoked at the beginning of all well-known devotions to Mary; it is stamped in the Liturgy firmly fixed in the ancient anthem—*Sub tuum praesidium*—that shelters all Christian communities under her patronage. A copy of this prayer was found in the third century; an evidence that St. Agnes, St. Cecilia, St. Cyrian and Origen used it exactly as we do. Running to her for refuge to hide under her mantle has endured for almost two thousand years.

Years of controversial struggle were concluded when the Oecumenical Council of Ephesus pronounced the definition; this marked a turning point in the unfolding (often dramatic) of Mariology. That definition was as important to the early Christians as the definition of the Immaculate Conception was for us in our time. The Church acknowledged the greatest title of Mary's nobility, that of Mother of God, from which logically all her other titles are derived.

That definition was only the springtime of development; the flower was still in the bud but the heat of controversy would open it. There was no question of the definition being an innovation in Christianity, nor was it a spiritual invention; it was in reality a jealous defense of the well-known and recognized prerogatives of a Woman—and such a WOMAN. In defending her, the Son is defended, because in defending His prerogatives, the Mother is protected. Mother and Son continue to be associated, one with the other, even by those who oppose her.

The Nestorian heresy made it evident that no one can attack the attributes of Mary without diminishing belief in the divinity of Christ; similarly, no one can lessen the divinity of Christ without harm to the great role played by the Virgin Mother.

When at last her children were freed from the narrow views of men, fearful of the miraculous (and these were the first to deny her) Mary, like a marvelous flower has blossomed in Christian hearts, filled Christian homes with her fragrance, and made firesides a place of contentment. She has her place in Christian temples of worship, and there she listens to the tales of suffering, to the aspirations of hope, and receives the intimate confidences of her children. The deepest affections, the boldest ambitions, the most daring secret plans are all laid on her bosom—the bosom that bore Jesus—and with them a coronal of thanks.

Her image is found in the beautifully appointed rich chapels, in poor wayside shrines, in niches between the forked branches of a tree, in home statues and icons, on medals and in paintings. She is pictured in the gilded tympanums above the entrances of a cathedral and in mortuary chapels; everywhere she gathers together the love and hopes of men, nourishing the very faculty for love in this iron age that has catapulted the world into a menacing cloud of hate.

In a word, Christian people understood at once that she was restoring divine Motherhood to mankind, just as Jesus had restored the divine Fatherhood of God to them. There was, perhaps, another reason for the silence of the first centuries concerning Mary. Christianity was in its infancy and, according to St. Paul's figure of speech, "still fed at the breast." An infant is carried in its mother's arms, although it has no definite consciousness of this. The instinct of life draws a babe to those twin founts of motherly nourishment; he has almost no other need but that of food. As his life unfolds with time, he learns to recognize his mother's face and smile, loving her in her care and in herself.

Similarly, Christianity was hungry, seeking Christ to be fed by Him, thus unconscious of Mary's motherly arms that carried the Infant Church. As Christianity grew, it became aware of its sonship by adoption, which makes every baptized man a brother of Christ; it also makes him a son of the Virgin Mary because a son of the Heavenly Father. Christians, logically, became conscious of her Motherhood, hence their love for Mary grew with the years. Love for her continues to grow. It has traveled a long road, from Ephesus to the Vatican, from the grotto of Bethlehem to that of Lourdes; from the simple statement of Hippolitus to the Mariology of St. Bernard.

The Mother and her Children

Mary had been saluted by the Archangel as "full of grace"; God Himself had spoken to her through His ambassador. Destined to be the Mother of Jesus, she would be the Mother of grace. She had been prepared by Heaven to open upon earth a fountain of grace. And this she did from the moment of the Annunciation onwards. Elizabeth had been flooded with a superhuman joy at seeing her; because of her aid, the newly wedded couple at Cana kept their joy, so nearly turned to sorrow.

Her innocent hands purify whatever they touch. She touches the intellects of men and they are enlightened. Hearts open to her like buds freed from thorns; she awakens in them chaste thoughts, angelic aspirations, and heavenly tenderness. She touches sick bodies and they are cured; she has made all sacred and pure.

She manifests herself, and art springs up at her feet; she breathes, and the air is filled with song; she steps to the brink of suffering, and there hope and resignation waken. Her name is enough to cleanse a soul by driving away temptation and overcoming passion. Whatever is obscure, she clarifies; under her influence ugliness vanishes and beauty shines. Because of her, Nature itself is filled with joy as if under the caress of a rainbow. Nature, sharing in the fall of humanity, has regained something of its virginal beauty through her; and even the arid earth has smiled and thrilled at her name for twenty centuries.

Love has ever found new ways for her children to communicate with their Mother, and discovered many means for coming closer to her. None of their resources, however, have ever rivaled the popularity of the rosary, a humble chain of roses which embraces in its chaplet the whole cycle of mysteries in the Redemption and encloses heaven and earth in the totality of everything divine.

Prayerful souls use the rosary to draw near to God; God uses it to draw souls to himself. The rosary is Mary's ingenuity for bringing the redeemed in contact with the Redeemer.

Could anyone claim that the rosary is too simple a means for this? The reply is that we can do nothing about it, because God is simplicity itself, and He uses the most ordinary elements in His works. He takes a bit of clay and creates a man; He takes bread and changes it into His own Body; He takes wine, and by His power, it becomes His own Precious Blood. He Who made the planets and the stars has no need of a laboratory nor of thinking out scientific formulas.

The works of God may be incomprehensible to some intellectual exhibitionist, and yet they can be known and assimilated by the uneducated and illiterate ones. The mysteries of God are as simple as nature, even more so. The Gospel story is not unusual, and yet it contains marvelous mysteries.

What has been said of the rosary can be said of other devotions, equally popular, such as the Scapular of Mt. Carmel. A tiny piece of brown wool can represent a religious habit to the one who wears it and serve as a concrete sign of one's dedication to Mary. A person may be an outcast in the eyes of the world, but with her scapular he feels like a knight of his Lady Mary. He experiences some of the humble obedience which Grignion de Montfort felt when he dedicated himself to his Queen. He lives again the thrilling emotion of St. Ignatius of Loyola when he kept his great night watch with our Lady at Monserrat.

Such a man shares a little in the transports of lyric love with St. Bernard; and perhaps he too in his imagination dreams of her under the starry vaults of a cathedral. At any rate, the Scapular of Mt. Carmel has been worn by kings, and no one knows but what those in stern professorial ranks wear it; for the closer we come to the angelic way of loving, all self-importance is deflated; and before her, sovereigns, and those with scholastic degrees, discover that they are exactly like everyone else—her children.

KNIGHTS OF OUR LADY

The dramatic and adventurous period of the Middle Ages drew its inspiration from Mary. Monks built temples to her honor in important centers of Christianity or on isolated mountain heights; they built them on scenic elevations or hid them in the valleys, that all might see them from afar like so many fortresses of purity thrown as bridges between earth and heaven. These churches built in her honor were meeting places of piety; to them the faithful, weary of weapons or the plow, ascended or descended, if not by foot, at least by prayerful sighs and desires. Often, only a glance towards her sanctuary home would check an angry gesture and renew a soul.

Sea merchants, when setting sail on some new enterprise, were accustomed to set apart the choicest of the merchandise they would acquire for her. If the Church was built to Mary in the center of the city, their thoughts turned wistfully towards it as to the home where the Mother of all men waited and watched for them; so that, when far away under unknown skies, on stormy nights, they would invoke her with the confidence of little children calling to their mother in the dark.

When the merchants returned they would vie with their neighbors in embellishing her dwelling; making of it a royal palace, all marble, gold and mosaics, where Jesus would dwell, the Son with the Mother, and they felt closer and more intimate with Both. So cities vied with one another in choosing her as patron. Republics were dedicated to her. Her feast day was the signal for a community holiday of joy, and from family treasure chests would come silks, candles and jewels to honor her—the All-Pure One. Religious orders were dedicated to her and bore her name; not just a few, but *all* considered themselves as coming from her; families of virgins mystically begotten by the Virgin Mother.

Kings consecrated their crowns to her. The cult of devotion to the Virgin Mother of God is very ancient and extensive in Italy. It is expressed by many, many shrines, feasts, customs, confraternities under her title; it has inspired numerous marvels of painting on canvas, on marbles, and masterpieces of sculptured beauty. Works of piety and faith have sprung up that may be said to be innate in Italian genius from the beginning of Christianity. For the Italians, the Blessed Virgin is one of the family, always loved and never forgotten. She is spoken of with a joyful and a kind of jealous sweetness, as of a person with whom one is always on intimate terms. For centuries, saints, and sovereigns, humble folk, and soldiers have gone on pilgrimage to her shrines, to Rome, to Loretto, and elsewhere, telling her of their love and offering her their services.

They return home with her gifts to them of renewed purity and faith, on which to build acts and deeds of goodness. I do not believe there is in Italy a city, village or hamlet that is not, in one way or another, dedicated to Mary, and does not believe itself loved by her. At one time England was Called "Mary's Dowry." After centuries of conflict against Moslem domination, the Reconquest of Spain was won at the battle of Covadonga, and here a sanctuary to the Blessed Virgin was erected, her first church in Spain. In tragic hours St. Stephen of Hungary dedicated his kingdom to her. Sovereigns and warriors were willing to fight for such a Lady; to purify their motives for war by love of that Heavenly Queen.

The nations of Europe have all placed themselves under the patronage of Our Lady, and they are still hers, except for those periods of war, madness and destruction. In France's hour of military catastrophe, old Marshal Petain recommended his country to the Virgin of Lourdes. Millions of mothers in the warring continents entrusted their sons to Mary's care.

Towards the close of the Middle Ages, the incentive for voyages and for war, that had found full vent in the Crusades, now gave place to ocean adventures in quest of new lands. The large majority started out like knights, going to unknown lands for love of their ladies, and boldly sailed across the wide seas out of love for the Madonna, trusting themselves to her.

Portugal, with its long line of navigators, believed itself born of the love of our Lady of Bethlehem, whose shrine was near the port of Lisbon, a place of arrival and departure, consequently, a place of national glory. It is still standing, a poem in stone. Her Portuguese children still sing the "Lusiad," their great epic poem.[5] Portuguese explorers moved towards the unknown for the sake of faith and the empire. God was their pilot; Mary was their star. Before they set sail, they knelt at the altar of the Madonna as did Vasco da Gama.

---

[5] "The Lusiad"—a Portuguese epic poem by Camoens, celebrating the voyage of Vasco da Gama in 1497, that opened the route to India by way of the Cape of Good Hope. "The Lusiad" was published in 1571.

He spent the night preceding his voyage, keeping the vigil of a knight over his arms with the Madonna whom he had chosen for his Lady. Cabral, the discoverer of Brazil, did the same.

It may be thought that in our present times, chivalrous and adventurous love has declined and faded away under the disintegrating influence of vulgar passions mingled with narrow-minded politics. But behold, the Blessed Virgin has spoken again to the Portuguese people, as well as to humanity everywhere, by appearing to three simple children at Fátima. Today, Fátima rises like another receiving station of universal love for Mary.

At Mary's altar, Magellan and Christopher (Christ bearer) Columbus prayed before weighing anchor to set sail on their voyages. The medieval world of chivalry fell apart with Don Quixote after the great enterprise of Columbus in discovering a new world. The English prince, Astolfo, a knight in Charlemagne's court, would have considered Columbus a very practical man, who could overcome monsters of the sea and on the land. But the adventure of Columbus was inspired and enlightened by the most beautiful and purest of women, to whom his chivalrous soul looked as to the summit of his ideals, Mary. She had tamed and civilized the wild nomads of the Middle Ages; inspired art and poetry, as well as sponsoring the most daring and fascinating adventures.

When the American people begin to react against their mechanical progress and stock-market operations (and the signs point now to this time) and turn with greater interest to poetry and art, they will find in the beginnings of their civilization an abundance of epic material and can draw from it a great literature. This WOMAN, crowned with a diadem of stars, will hold an eminent place. Like a most clear star, she will be the goal as well as the source of all their most daring aspirations. She will often be found to be their unique source of comfort and courage on a tempest-tossed ocean, in land racked by hunger, thirst, by disease or by a host of enemies.

"O admirable commercium," exclaims Daniel Sargent, one of the first initiators of this epic literature in the United States. A Calvinist, he was brought to the starry port of Mother Church by his love for Mary. That text, so expressive of the relation between this heroic convert and Mary, between the new world and the Mother of redeemed men, is written as the title of his book "Our Land and Our Lady." Sargent writes, "In our beginning it was the *Santa Maria* that sailed towards our shores—Columbus's *Santa Maria*, Queen Isabella's *Santa Maria*, Castile's *Santa Maria*, Christendom's *Santa Maria*." [6]

Christianity was sending the *Santa Maria* with a handful of heroes—Christophers—"Christ bearers," to conquer a new world and ease the breathing of the old world, feeble and exhausted with age. "The *Santa Maria* brought the Incarnation to the new world"; at the same time giving a discoverer to America. This strangest of all discoverers was well suited to discover the strangest of all lands. "The most paradoxical land that Christendom has yet produced looks to a discoverer who presents ever for its thoughts the complete human paradox, and, more significant, the complete human Christian paradox." [7]

Every evening, the crew that accomplished this great adventure, sang the "Salve Regina," and by that prayer, time was divided. The "Salve Regina" marked the pause between day and night. Christopher Columbus belonged so much to the Blessed Virgin that he blended her initials with his own signature, and specified that when he died he should be buried in the chapel of the Immaculate Conception in the

---

[6] "Our Land and Our Lady," by Daniel Sargent, Chap. I.
[7] *Ibid.*

valley called the Conception, in Haiti. In this way did the Mother of God take possession of America. Mother of God, venerated in her spotless Conception.

Following the trail opened by Columbus there came other cavaliers and adventurers of all kinds, some in quest of new lands for their king, some seeking gold for themselves. Among the cavaliers were the real knights of Christ and of the Blessed Virgin, who were seeking, neither lands nor gold, but only for new men. They came to conquer new souls for Christ the King. Dominicans, Franciscans, Augustinians, Jesuits and missionaries of other orders old and new, mingled with that crowd of conquistadores and seekers of riches. These missioners for Christ saw to it that true adventure was not lost in a frenzied search for gold, that it was not a plundering invasion of Satan, but rather the beginning of a great portentous episode in evangelization. That was the same century when St. Francis Xavier left Rome to visit the sanctuary of the Virgin at Loretto, to take leave of that Blessed One before starting out in his great Christian conquest.

In this way the Indians in the New World received baptism and learned new Christian ways of life. Their land was cultivated. New cities sprang up in the wake of pioneers who penetrated virgin forests and dank marshes, and in their toilsome marches kindled the light of that name, more beautiful than any other.

Father Marquette, the explorer of that regal river, the Mississippi, drifted along its water on a raft singing the office he had composed in honor of Mary Immaculate. His trust in her had encouraged him to undertake this most strange and perilous expedition.

Despite violence, martyrdom, and setbacks due to ignorance and to heresy, the building up of the New World was accomplished with the inspiration and help of Mary. A tribe of Indians, the Flat-heads, called their mission and village

"St. Mary." The missionaries succeeded in convincing thousands of redskins (now driven from their native soil) that their only reliable refuge, a refuge faithful to her promises, was the Mother of God, AUXILIUM ET REFUGIUM INDIANORUM.[8] Thus placed in the heart of the New World, the Blessed Virgin has remained there.

Henry Adams, a Puritan, by dint of his studies in the history of civilization, had to admit that the only alternative, for civilization or for himself, was to be faithful to the Blessed Virgin or to be unfaithful to Christ; and in his heart—as his poetry shows—he was faithful to her. This fidelity is the one unique way remaining to humanity, if humanity is to advance.

The true way, because it leads to Mary, leads to reverence of the human person and to Christian happiness; the other way, opposed to Mary, leads to sectarianism and infidelity, because it rejects the supernatural in religion; it teaches not only the discarding of the last traces of Calvinism but also of the liberal Christianity that has taken its place. It leads, as Henry Adams saw clearly, to a deified dynamo; and the cult of this new civilization would be the cult of blind force.

---

[8] Help and refuge of all Indians.

11. *Nazareth*

The Virgin Mother
of Poetry

Come, Virgin of virgins,
Come, Light of lights,
Come, Fount of pardon.[1]

POETS OF THE MADONNA

The last one of the "Contes de la Vierge," written by the Tharaud brothers, tells about the Eucharist. The book ends with these words, "Perhaps, dear reader, you will ask where the Virgin is found in this tale? I answer you, she is wherever poetry is found." Mary is poetry. The most perfect poetry will awaken in the mind of the reader a thought of the Virgin; because it will have a perfection that reflects her beauty.

In the early centuries of Christianity, Christian souls, barely freed from persecutions and the difficulties of Christological controversies, sought rest in poetry and found there their greatest inspiration—the Madonna. A theologian almost inadvertently passes from his dry treatise into verse, from history into ballad, especially when he enters the radius of her purity. To those logical minds aflame with polemics, to those souls seeking to scale the ladders of the mystical life, she will come with lightsome fingers to loosen from the

---

[1] "Veni, virgo virginum
Veni, lumen luminum
Veni, vena veniae"   A.H. 54,250:1.

142

hearts' enclosure that strain of emotion which bursts into lyric praise.

In pronouncing her name they pass from the aridity of dialectics to the heights on which the variegated lights of grace shine, and from there they see the horizon that arches out into the virginal dawn. Memory flowers with fantasy and images burst into expression like clusters of stars in a soft blue sky. The soul, that a moment before trembled as it gazed into the abyss of mystery, is now enchanted with the beauty of Mary. She is the star of the sea; some compare her to a moon wandering in the dark solitudes of the soul; others delight in her fragrance as delicate as that of an early rose.

In the West after the Church had emerged out of the catacombs and the first cathedrals were built, strains of poetry were heard for the first time; hymns of praise to Christ; then Mary's name was interwoven in the history of the miracle from which Christ blossomed. That spacious and noble soul, St. Ambrose, in a hymn he wrote, asks the Redeemer to reveal to us the beauty of the virgin birth.[2] Later, the voice of Sedulius is heard as the herald of Mary, exalting the blessedness of her womb where the joys of Motherhood are united with the honor of virginity, because Mary pleased Christ above all other women.

In the East, St. Ephrem, a few years older than St. Ambrose, composed many hymns to the Virgin in the Syriac language. These were used in the Christmas liturgy. In them, the Church, from Persia to Brittany, never wearies of telling her wonderment and thanks for the gift that the Mother of the God-Man made to us.

> The Virgin bids me sing of her graces,
>   at which I marvel.

---

[2] Veni, Redemptor gentium
   Ostende partum Virginis,
   Miretur omne saeculum:
   Talis decet partus Deum. Inno. VIII str.2.

> O Son of God, give me your admiration
>   with your gift,
> And portray the image of Your Mother,
> So filled with beauty.

And the poet St. Ephrem sang with the heart of one who regarded Mary as "the paradise of God."

At the heights of his polemics against the Iconoclasts, St. John Damascene, inspired by the loveliness of Mary, called her "the glory of the priesthood," the "Queen of Nature," and frequently invoked her thus: "O lily, among thorns, O rose among the briers, shed your fragrance over all things." And he speaks of the aureole of stars around her head; for him, she was the WOMAN seen by St. John, the contemplative, in the Apocalypse.

Oriental poetry presented her under the aspect of *power*, always picturing a magnificent court where majesty was exalted above anything human; where the women with their charms exercised more power than men. So the Orientals called Mary, Queen, Empress, Most Exalted Lady. . . .

Meanwhile, the Middle Ages were drawing to a close in a luminous night in which the bloody birth of a new civilization was taking place. Anxious minds in the castles of nobles, in monasteries hidden in valleys or perched isolated and alone on mountain crags, on cliffs overlooking the sea, everywhere —even to the borders of the unknown—*all* were turning to Mary, seeking her heavenly aid and light. It was a period of iron, and men yearned for womanly gentleness; a lonely period, when men were orphans and sought for a mother. Above all, in the sixth century, Christianity sang with a full voice to Mary, repeating the petition of Venantius Fortunatus, "Jesus, flower of the Virgin Mother, come to our aid."

New poetry is always inspired by true womanhood, and above all it is born at the feet of the Madonna. The first impulse ascends to Mary, then it goes out to other women on earth as by a reflex action. The Middle Ages sang of its own love for Mary in numberless stanzas, in endless repetition, repeating her praises and giving us to understand that, for the most part, men lived by that love and found in it the joy of living and the strength to die; begging with wounded Orlando:

"Do thou succour me, O holy Mary!"

Devotion to her is universal. It is as if, in having reached her virginal light, all quarrels cease, all differences are ended. All suddenly find themselves her children and brothers, under her outstretched mantle.

If it is night, it is a night that Mary's love brightens with the Light of the Word. A Cistercian monk wrote of her exuberantly.

"Florida, rorida, lucida, fulgida, lumine digna!"[3]

"Flowering, dewy, shining, brilliant, noble light."

If Christ is the sun, Mary is the moon that is never eclipsed; a moon that has generated the sun. For centuries men never wearied of telling her praises. St. Albert of Cologne remarked, "We must never cease our service to her, nor our praise of her."

The seed of praise brought to earth by the Archangel fell into the hearts of generations who loved her, and produced a smiling vegetation like an immense forest in bloom, full of song to the sun (Christ) and to the moon (Mary).

Each song of praise for Mary awakens a desire to draw nearer to her; to ascend closer to her who dwells in expressible light. It is love that draws one, and the more one sings of her, the more is one's heart inflamed with love. This song of love seems to be something common to the majority of Christian people. Most of the hymns written to her are anonymous and are often variations of the same theme. This is al-

---

[3] Anon. Noanus, Cistercian Monastery, twelfth or thirteenth centuries. A.H. 48,298; 11, V.8.

ways a sign that they were sung by the people: the same
people who built the great basilicas. This is the reason Christianity rests in the arms of Mary, or runs to her for protection.

Religious Orders, Confraternities, cities and nations are
represented in art as covered in their widest limits under her
heavenly mantle which, resting on the shoulders of this
maiden, is spread out by her two frail hands to cover them
all.

It is the instinct of youthful society to yearn for a mother;
so in her arms society finds light, gladness and strength. Those
who leave their Father's house sometimes forget her and are
ungrateful; but in the dark hours of trouble, they sigh for the
warmth of that home—the Church—and long for her sweet
smile that never holds the least shadow of deceit.

The poets, when singing the praises of God, of Jesus in His
glory or in His sufferings, the perfections of the Saints, in-
variably find a way in which to mention Mary. She is always
present where the glory of God scintillates, where the Saints
love, and where poetry lives. There is no more powerful or
effective prayer to Jesus than the title, "Son of Mary." It is
the title of His birth and His honor; with one swift stroke
it brings Him to our level, to our condition as men and
brothers, one human family; while for her sake He shows
Himself full of loving pity for all.

Truly, the Middle Ages sang their songs of love to this
maiden of Jesse. Books of songs embrace all those found in
the Liturgy, in the Schools, in the ancient drawings in the
catacombs, by the hermits in their caves, and in verses composed by the itinerant friars. Naturally, they all contemplated
her chastity and her motherhood, for they had, as we have,
the greatest need of both.

In the books about Mary that have been preserved for us,
so abundant in figures, symbols, titles and poetry, the hymns

to the Virgin form by themselves a section richer than all the others together; and this was not because Mary came between God and men, but because her children called on her to be led by her hand to God. They believed that the sure way to the Son was by way of the Mother; the Bridegroom by way of the Bride; to the Father by the hand of the Daughter. Mary is still the handmaid of Divinity at the service of humanity.

Thus it was. We must not be surprised at this continual versification in honor of Mary. As an anonymous writer sang, "Through her we have God for our Brother."

This effect of Mary's maternity has deeply impressed Christian society. We received from Mary, in a visible, concrete way, the fruit of our Redemption. We are made brothers of Jesus, through Mary; therefore, as the theologian poet, St. Anselm of Canterbury, used to say, "Our Judge is our brother; the Saviour of the world is our brother; and finally, God has become our Brother through Mary." [4]

Confronted with this fact, the glorification of the most blessed Virgin comes spontaneously. "No one is equal to Mary; no one outside of God is greater than Mary. . . . Every nature was created by God, and the God-Man was born of Mary. God created all things, and Mary generated the God-Man. God Who can do all things, made Himself from Mary, and thereby he re-made all the things He had made. . . . God, therefore, is Father of created things, and Mary is mother of things re-made." [5]

It is Mary, who—so to speak—detaches the Three Divine Persons of the Trinity from their superhuman heights and presents them to us as our kith and kin, our brothers, she being the Mother of God and ours also. "Our sister and our Patron."

---

4 St. Anselm—Orat. 52—P.L. 158, 957.
5 Ibid. P.L. 158, 956.

> So near, so humble,
> Rejoice, pure maiden,
> You rule Him who is the Ruler.

And still she remains so high, so powerful and so resplend-
ant.

> The empress of queens,
> Repairer of our life,
> Fruitful olive;
> Precious pearl, violet, lily and rose,
> A flower immortelle.[6]

In this collection of poetic figure and verse, all is not
poetry. Much of it is school-boy writing. There was plenty of
naïveté and absence of art, but love which is the heart of art
was rarely if ever found missing.

There are many plays on words, assonances with difficult
variations, sincere or pretended playfulness; an evidence of
what the poets were thinking.

> Drop of nectar, star of the sea,
> Your sweetness is sweeter than honey,
> Your light brighter than the stars.
> Ladder of heaven, school of all good,
> You shed the sun, O Virgin,
> Alone both Virgin and Mother.[7]

Here is a sort of ladder to climb up to her:

Ave pia,   *Ave parens,*
Ave via,   *Labe carens,*
Ave vitis,   *Ave rosa;*
Ave mitis,   *Speciosa,*
Ave suavissima   *Ave, splendidissima.*[8]

---

[6] A.H. 1. 86,4.
[7] A.H. 8, 87, 1.
[8] A.H. 42, 103.

A floral poet saw in Mary "the origin of gardens," just as others saw in her "the Flower of flowers."

POETS OF THE FIRST RENAISSANCE

St. Peter Damian calls Mary the "ladder of Heaven," connecting the world with God. His poetry flowered in the troublesome times of the eleventh century, after Christian spirituality had at last gained some autonomy and pre-eminence over temporal things through the epoch-making efforts of Hildebrand. St. Mary's aide, St. Peter Damian's verses become delicate and lovely; at the same time they reveal his vigorous temperament, as when he invokes her against a hail storm:

> O Merciful One, O powerful Queen,
> Command with a word
> That we be not devastated
> By these clattering stones of hail! [9]

He attributes to Mary a power which he calls "a vast pontificate" capable of saving humanity from storms.

St. Anselm, that southern light in the cold country of the North, writing at the dawn of the twelfth century after Hildebrand's reform had brought about a new spring of spiritual life, a civil and artistic renaissance in Christian Europe, saw Mary in the light of divinity.

> Having divinity generating in her,
> She nourishes humanity,
> And develops it.

St. Peter the Venerable, when invoking Christ, the Son of God, turns his thoughts to the Mother, and exclaims:

---

[9] O miseratrix, O dominatrix, praecipe dictus
ne devastemur, ne lapidemur grandidis ictu.

> Remember Christ, Who you are,
> And why You had the Virgin for a mother——
> That You might save humanity.[10]

And the saint continues to remind the Son of the Mother's milk, her kisses, her caresses and her tears: "a Mother in the fullest sense of the word." A Mother with a mother's trust. Again he sings of the drops of her milk that can quench the fires of hell.

There were some poets who composed variations of the AVE MARIA, of the MAGNIFICAT, and other liturgical hymns; they wove the long lists of her attributes into poetical strands; some built of them lofty towers of lapis lazuli with mosaic stairs. Others sang of the blessedness of every part of her person; of her robes, the steps she took, the sandals on her feet. They made love to her seated on a throne, caressing her hands and kissing her rings, whilst they prayed an Ave Maria over each. All this was done in the spirit of filial veneration, pure and refined. "Blessed ever will be the milk that fed Him Who feeds the faithful with Himself in the Eucharist," they would say. And while some wept at the thought of her many sorrows, others rejoiced over each joy that the Blessed Virgin, "Cause of our Joy," has given us.

St. Bernard, that militant knight, the minstrel of Mary, summarized what had already been said and formulated many other things for the first time. From the cold frozen forests of the North countries [11] Alexander Neckman, who died in 1227, salutes Mary with verses of singular beauty.

> Thou art life of the world,
> And gate of heaven;
> Luster of Sharon and of Carmel,

---

[10] Recordare quis et quare Matrem habes virginem:
   Causa nota est et tota ut salvares hominem.
[11] These references to countries of the North mean England, Germany, Belgium, Holland, etc.

> The halo of virgins.
> Bright with rays of light
> From on high,
> Thou art the center
> Of heat in our winter.

Dante, climaxing all this construction of love, although praying through the voice of St. Bernard, intones his hymn to the Virgin Mother that crowns his great Paradiso, invoking her, as we do on our death beds, to open to us the door into Eternal Love. She is the watchword for entering into the Vision of God.

> O Virgin Mother, daughter of thy Son,
> Created beings all in lowliness
> Surpassing, as in height above them all:
> Term by the eternal Council pre-ordained
> Ennobler of thy nature, so advanced
> In thee, that its great Maker did not scorn
> Himself in His own work enclosed to dwell.

In these verses of such strong soaring, the poet gathers together all the prophecies of the patriarchs, the definitions of the theologians, the aspirations of the mystics, and sums up in them all the songs of hope and love of Christians. In this pageantry poetry comes to a halt; it could not go beyond Poetry itself.

At that time, Jacopone da Todi whose ascetic ideals plunged him into many a wordy battle with the mediocre and who in his passion gave vent to sarcasm and bitter invectives, thrilled at the sight of Mary with the Infant Jesus in her arms, and wept at the sight of Jesus on the Cross with Mary standing near. He has given expression to his emotion in the most tender and tragic of songs. His accents still fill modern souls with sincere emotions.

In his verse the Virgin speaks and acts, while Jacopone

shares with her her indescribable joys and sorrows. His LAUDA
is full of a dramatic action that wrings tears from the eyes
and effects a real conversion of soul. She sees her Son crowned
with thorns. and she weeps in anguish and love, as all mothers
would do.

> Son, Son, my Son,
> My most adorable lily!

And when He died, she murmurs:

> Son, Thy soul is gone from Thee.
> Son of a bewildered Mother,
> Son of a vanquished Mother,
> My afflicted Son.
>
> White and ruddy is my Son,
> Without resemblance to other men,
> O my Son, to Whom I cling,
> And yet, Thou hast abandoned me!

With Petrarch, love seemed to return from explorations
and discoveries which had greatly enlightened men and times,
dogmas and the proofs of faith, exposing the errors and delusions of earthly love; then the whole Church gathered together in a lyric prayer, her last and purest quest after a
femininity of transparent virginity and divine womanhood. In
Petrarch, the singer of Laura, poetry, because touching the
divine, becomes more human and more luminous.

> Three names Thou linkest, that are
>   sweet and dear,
> Mother and Child and Bride;
> O Virgin glorified,
> Queen of that Lord Who, to this
>   earthly sphere,

> Loosing our bonds, brought
> liberty and bliss.

Whenever poets sing of the Virgin, they rise to the heights of pure Poetry. In touching her, they touch Poetry. So it was with Petrarch, his lyric, concluding with Mary, becomes terse and brief. Boccaccio too, becomes transfigured when he speaks of her. He breathes an inspiration worthy of an angel. At about the same time, Chaucer, that genial, smiling father of English literature, wrote some glowing verses of Mary (who always inspires one with love for her), and tells of his faith in her Immaculate Conception. He had his portrait painted with a rosary in his hand, to let us know the path of his poetic inspiration that traveled from earth to Heaven. Chaucer was ever a poet and loving son of Mary.

In a Carthusian monastery at Prague, about the middle of the fourteenth century, Conrad of Haimberg sang sweetly and tenderly of Mary. Many have imitated his love and his style ever since. His hermit cell literally sparkled with poetic gems about Mary, and his verses are crowded with her beautiful titles. He was most original and unique in his canticles of love to her, singing of her clothing, the ribbon in her hair, the ring on her finger, and the throne on which he seated her.

In his poem "The Banquet of the Most Sweet Virgin Mary," he addresses her:

> O Mary, spouse of our Lord,
> Who, for man's salvation
> Was divinely given——
> Like a rose joined to a lily,
> Together with thy Son
> Thou art called
> To Eternal nuptials.[12]

---

[12] "Maria, sponsa Domini, quae in salutem homini divinitus es data, Una cum tuo filio ut rosa juncta lilio ad nuptias vocata."

Christian humanity, whose sufferings were now purified
by grace, understood the human sufferings of Christ, its Head,
and lamented Him at the foot of the Cross on Calvary's hill-
top, pouring out the flood of its sorrow with Mary in the
Stabat Mater.

> At the cross her station keeping,
> Stood the mournful Mother weeping,
> Close to Jesus to the end.

SONGS OF THE NEW AGE

Next comes humanism. Written poetry struggled, smoth-
ered by style. Filial love for Mary seemed to die under the
outbursts of pride. The Church's social consciousness in the
home and family began to fall apart, so that in the hearts of
many Christians a feeling for the Mother is lost. In part of
Christianity the family is missing so there is no place for the
Mother. Those who rebelled against the Church rebelled
against her, and where there is no love for Our Lady, base
instincts multiply, and the home is supplanted by the cellular
custom of people living apart and alone.

When the "De partu Virginis" of Sannazzaro appeared, the
stylists thought that Mariology had inspired, at long last, the
national poem of a Christian Aeneid. Alas, it was poetry more
vergilian than virginal, embellished with graceful rhetoric
rather than with true poetic genius. And it ended up in the
crypts of libraries, stowed away with other piles of vergilian
verse and curious compositions written for the sake of a sheer
penmanship hobby.

Happily, love for Mary continued to sing in the hearts of
the saints: not only in the hearts of canonized saints but also

in the hearts of numberless of the humble, who remained faithful to the love that constitutes sanctity, amidst the deafening noise of pagan and rebellious doctrines.

In the midst of his controversial writings and dogmatic excavations, St. Robert Bellarmine, turned to Mary and, like a child again, sang:

> O Virgin, fair as a red rose,
> On my heart repose!

Tired of arguing, he sought peace in love and beauty, and in his heart the Virgin transformed dogma into poetry.

In the hours of religious fervor, the singing city of Naples, during the missions preached by St. Francis Jerome, sang with all its soul a paraphrase of the SALVE REGINA composed by the Saint. It was heard from the roaring seashores to the slums, blending in one the voices of virgins consecrated to God, women converted from their sinful ways of life, half-naked urchins, and the bourgeois with their hats on their heads.

> Hail, Queen and universal Mother,
> Through whose favor we climb to Heaven.
> You are the joy and the smile of all the
>   disconsolate,
> The only hope of all the desperate.

And in that sacred song, the Naples of the sixteenth century found laughter and joy springing from a fountain of hope.

Thus St. Alphonsus Maria De Liguori, putting down his stylus of theological speculation and discussion, gave free rein to his emotion in some graceful stanzas and composed his "Glories of Mary." Christians innumerable have repeated his praises of Mary in many languages.

No one can say how many poets have written for themselves, or longed to write of this most desirable Mother, especially when they think of death approaching. Joachim Belli, after writing sonnets like arrows sharp with irony and anger, turns to Mary as the one and only person who has never deceived him; and commenting on her Litany in loving tercets, he says:

> O morning star of hope,
> To the infirm, thou art health;
> To the sinner, the only refuge left in the world.
>
> To Christians, an efficacious help;
> To angels, their most beautiful Queen,
> Crowned with stars and vested with the sun.
> . . . .
> Sweet Mother Mary, pray for us.[14]

Little by little, amidst songs interspersed with much hatred and equally as much with forgetfulness of this Mother, we come, in our times, to the chaste imagery of Manzoni and the virginal invocations of Mistral. Although Carducci marks the end of the Italian Renaissance, the verses of this poet of pagan ideas conclude in accents of love for the Virgin Mary. In comparison to her, his unbelieving and liberal Muse pales like the light of a star.

> Ave Maria! When the air resounds,
> With the humble salutation,
> Little mortals bare their heads;
> Bow their foreheads,
> Dante and Harold.

Life sinks to its sunset time. And death, even for the poet, draws near with the insecurity of old age. The smoke of

---

[14] "Litany of the Blessed Virgin"—popular edition.

youthful ambitions fades away; then the poet, like others, feels his soul awakened and, tired, he sighs for home, and within that home that most sweet Mother in whom all Poetry is completed and made eternal.

So, in the life of the poet, Mary is victorious at the end over Satan. Barres, vexed that his Catholicity was doubted, protested, "I love the holy Virgin very much," intending to imply by that, "If any one loves this Mother—and such a Mother—he loves the Son also and all that belongs to Him." [15]

Among contemporary poets, not a few have in moments of clear inspiration felt the need of Mary, and have written many beautiful verses in her honor, Musicians have composed many sweet variations of AVE MARIA. It will suffice to quote two stanzas of Sister Madeleva—a Sister from the prairies of Indiana—and a poet.[16] One is to St. Bernard:

> Mary is the flower-field, where
> Bernard, the bee,
> Drinks wild nectar to
> Ecstasy.

One is to St. Dominic:

> Dominic, the dog, his
> Mouth aflame,
> Is a firebrand lighted at
> Mary's name.

---

[15] This is related by François Mauriac in "Mes Premières Années à Paris" (*Le Figaro*, March 23, 1940).
[16] Sister M. Madeleva, C.S.C. St. Mary's College, Notre Dame, Indiana.

12. *Nazareth*

Mother of God
and Mother of Men

Saint of all Saints, Virgin Theotokos,
The Mother of God, foremost of all mothers;
She, first and alone, has glorified the feminine sex,
Queen of all men and Queen of all women.
                              ST. JOHN DAMASCENE—P.G.96,809.

ART'S OFFERING TO MARY

As the beginnings of modern Christian literature and the richest veins of poetry were formed around Mary, so other forms of art kept pace with them; seeking in her their purest expression and drawing from her their richest inspiration. This is not surprising, since she is poetry, she is beauty.

The most beautiful figures in painting—divinely beautiful —are representations (only approximate, alas,) of her beauty, and the eminence of the great artists was stimulated by their ardent desire to envision her, and to fix on canvas some of her characteristics as Virgin, as Mother, while praying or while suffering.

It is seldom that Jesus is represented without the Mother, or the Virgin without the Son. At the Crib, at the Circumcision, at Cana, in the Passion, in Glory, she is always with Him and for Him: the trusted handmaid who neither abandons Him in life nor in death. In the "Assumption" of Titian, her gaze is completely absorbed in Him; it is His love that has drawn her heavenward. The crude art of the Ethiopians could never imagine her without the Child. An image of

158

Mary with the Child is for them, the Madonna: without the Child, she is an ordinary woman.

Our own art also prefers to present the Virgin with her Son. Seated with Him on her lap, she seems to be already on a throne. She holds on her knee her great title to royalty.

This representation expresses a consciousness that cannot separate the Son from His Mother. With a regal calm, proper to one who sustains God and is sustained by Him, she offers her Son to us. She supports Him and feeds Him while even now He smiles at us, plays and blesses men from His Mother's knee as from the seat of happiness; nor can there be anything so familiarly beautiful.

Without Mary, half the masterpieces in our art galleries would be missing; half of the joy of our days would disappear. More than half the great basilicas would never have risen to sing of the joy of having her for a sister, a mother and a friend. Catholic people should be characterized by their gaiety, in marked contrast to the somber attitude of the people among whom the cult of the Virgin is stifled. Our Churches are the scene of the Liturgy and the heart of the Liturgy is song; even when sad, it consoles, and almost always ends on a festive note. Feasts are celebrations which draw the faithful to the cathedrals where the Mother awaits her children with joy, to rejoice with them. *Genitrix laetitiae,* "Mother of Joy," Alexander Neckman calls her; and the Litany of Loretto acclaims her as "Cause of Our Joy." Thus she acts, especially towards those nations tried so sorely by miseries.

After the wreckage of the barbarian age, architecture revives, to erect, at Mary's request, some joyful cathedral above clumps of little houses. Following the impulse given by love for her and in the light of her purity, the lines of the edifice rise boldly; marbles become transparent to flower out into spiral scrolls, rose windows, arches pointing to heaven as if

to embrace it, and other symbols. Windows are hemmed
about with moulding resembling rich embroidery, to let in
the breath of life. The walls of these basilicas are made of
strong, square stones seeming less to rise out of the black
earth than to descend from the blue sky that envelops them.
They spread out in the sunshine like the mantle of the Madonna. The homes of Mary are found amidst the forests, and
on the prairies, towering above farmhouses like a sheer vision
of white.

Within, on the walls and columns, on the apses and in the
chapels, scenes from the life of Jesus are reproduced: His
Mother bending over His crib; or she is seen engaged in
manual work near a Boy Who is holding out tools to His
Father; or she is watching Him playing with doves near a
fountain. Or again, she is seen anxious at the wedding at
Cana, sorrowing at the foot of the cross, in the Cenacle with
the Apostles in retreat and giving witness to her own divine
maternity towards the Church. Finally, we see her asleep, then
flying heavenward in the Assumption; kneeling crowned as
Queen in the Presence of the Trinity surrounded by clouds
of angels.

Her womanly face, her motherly gestures give to the empty
space and solitary twilight a welcoming charm, a warmth of
family life which makes the Eucharistic Altar more intimate
and inviting—the Supper Table where the Son seems to come
to us by the hands of the Immaculate One; where all who receive the Son with a pure heart seem to renew once more the
miracle of Mary.

Heroines of the Old Testament, Sarah, Rachel, Deborah,
Esther and Judith stand out from the blood-stained background of ancient history to take on, near Mary, an atmosphere of being at home in the Church. They were strong,
sweet and dramatic persons, whom the *fiat* of Mary brought
into the realm of grace; and who, in the life of Mary, are

gathered together, for Eve had lost them and Mary found them again, just as the Son has gathered all humanity unto Himself.

She unites them to other women of whom she is the prototype—St. Agnes, St. Catherine, St. Joan of Arc, St. Theresa of Avila, St. Gemma Galgani, a feminine battalion of grace and fidelity; an escort to the might of the prophets and patriarchs—Abraham, Moses, Isaias, Micheas; to the genius and sacrifice of St. Paul, St. Ambrose, St. Augustine, St. Gregory and St. Francis.

Thus, Mary gathers together traditions and hopes, genius and power, she who is the strength of innocence.

> Thou art the beautiful Judith
> Who has freed the Church.

By their vows, the Saints gave themselves to Christ and to souls under Mary's protection. In the secrecy of their vigils, men of war or rigorous ascetics find their peace in Mary. In frescoes or in marble, one sees them represented in the shadow of her mantle, opened wide to receive every son of woman, every son of the Madonna.

Christendom is dotted with shrines of Mary like constellations in the sky. France has a shrine at Chartres where it is believed the Druids had erected a wooden statue to "the virgin who was to bring forth a son." Italy has one at Loretto, guarding the House of Nazareth. Germany, England, Greece, Spain, Poland, Bohemia, Slavonia and almost every country has built famous shrines, rich in gold and rich in piety to the Madonna. They have been great refuges for her children who hasten there to seek the aid of their mother; the goal of pilgrimages for the relief of misery and pain after pride has been deflated to its nothingness; a meeting place wherein to love and sing in the midst of the weariness of life. When all else is gone and only the Crucifix remains, we approach it with more confidence through the Mother who knew all His pain, and who was transfixed with seven swords of sorrow.

Her love extends to all; her motherhood is universal. And since every class of men claims her as its own, each builds a house to her, so that, abiding with all, she gives to all a universal service. In those Churches built in her honor, Christianity has consolidated its most beautiful and affectionate poetry for her; they are hymns in stone, as ethereal as the rainbow. In Mary's homes, wordly tempests beat and break against her pedestals and columns as against the stern of a ship; the sun shines within, nestling gaily among the pointed arches and pillars; doves build their nests in the decorative moulding on the face of the arches. Throngs of desires ascend to her from maidens and young men; they go to her when they marry and ask her to provide for them in their journey through life. Others, who wish to give themselves to God, pray to her that the doors of the cloister may open to them.

Multitudes of sailors turn their cargoes into gold and stones to build a Church in her honor. Men of agriculture promise that the first fruits of their brown furrows may be used to create a beautiful dwelling for her, so that she may stay near them. Towns and villages, states and nations wish to see her honored in temples and chapels, that divine mercy and supernatural poetry may not be wanting in their social life. She is like a Mother in their midst, sitting among her children, pacifying them and rejoicing with them.

"Our Lady" they call her; or Madonna "My Lady" because each one wishes to have her for himself and takes for granted that she feels for each. Where Mary is, there we meet those we love—our children, a mother, a maiden sister, a sweetheart or a nun, a spouse of Christ. Our thoughts take chaste flight through air that is pure; passions are dissipated, and out of the depths of man's wickedness, goodness leaps forth like a flame amidst the brambles. A sense of family unity returns with filial piety for Mary and brings art in its wake.

The Virgin Mother in Our Midst

Mary stands among Christians as the model of virginity and the model of motherhood, uniting in herself these two supreme attributes of womanhood. "O Mary, Mother of admirable virginity and Virgin of lovable fecundity." [18] "We adore the Virgin in the Mother of salvation." [19] Christian virgins are reflections of Mary. In seeing them, we see something of the Mother of God, continuing in them her work of graciousness, of consolation, of kindness and of prayer absorbed in God.

When we are in the midst of the world, we see nothing but the rush of those like ourselves, busy earning our daily bread (which is never sufficient); we hear those expressions of a hatred that brutalizes man and of an avarice that makes him so petty; we see the lust that makes men so filthy. Then, behold, some day in a hospital, in a school, or in a hidden monastery, we meet a Sister —*your* Sister, a nun who is a Spouse of Christ, whose daughter and handmaid she is.

Like Mary, hers is a daily exercise of contemplation, of prayer, and of charity; continually, she cuts out of her heart the tentacles of vanity, and makes of herself a lamp burning before God, giving light to men. If she speaks to you, you feel that her thoughts are pure, that her heart is fixed on Him Who is all purity; and Mary is, for her, the rule, the norm of chastity, the Forma Dei.

From what these religious say or do, one can understand

---

[18] St. Anselm, "Meditations and Prayers," Paris, 1922.
[19] Thus speaks a medieval poet in an outburst of lyric, but without any idolatrous intention (A.H. 45,6, P. 23). In this popular sense, non-theological, the locution is found also in St. Alphonsus Maria de Liguori.

the kind of woman Mary was: the Woman Who brought
forth Christ; for they likewise bring forth Christ unwearingly
among men and for men, by giving hospitality to the home-
less and by instructing the ignorant. For all the calumnies
they receive, they give only goodness in return, a soft light
of sweet chastity, a sense of purity; and they satisfy the need
of love that dissolves the crust of rancor; then the soul lifts
its heavy burdens, revives and loves once more. Mary, Mother
of Virgins!

These daughters of Mary love with the devotion and the
sense of sacrifice so proper to women; from Mary's example
they have lifted this love to alpine heights where it becomes
purer, without shadow of flesh or tainted with the effects of
life's low regions. They love humanity in Christ as Mary
loved it. One sees them, like clear flames, burning as lamps
before the Blessed Sacrament in the shadows and in silence.
These are the virgins espoused to Mary's Son.

Their relation to others is that of supernatural motherhood, in which they bend with unwearying love over every
misery; servants of all because they see in all the Body of
Christ Whom they serve. They give us the image of the virginal motherhood and the motherly virginity of Mary, handmaid of the Lord, whose "blessed virginity consecrates all
chastity, and whose glorious generating saves all fruitful-
ness." [20]

These consecrated women represent all this; and if the
flow of human passions and instincts seems to dash against
their silent convents, it breaks and clears, for their virginity
virginizes and their sacrifice redeems. Modeled exactly on the
example of Mary and of her Son, the Church has cultivated
with jealous care the miraculous flower of virginity, which
distills a sweet consolation to all. It is the filter in which the
exchange of human affections is continually purified.

---

[20] St. Anselm. *op. cit.*, p. 18.

The Church, in consecrating them to God and to their neighbor, thus freeing them from bonds with one particular person, destines them to the service of the entire community of the faithful; and this service may be entirely of prayer and suffering, or of prayer and an apostolate of various means for helping others. And this consecrated life of the vows prevents them at once from growing hard, into a sort of exclusiveness, or walling up self in a kind of ascetic aristocracy. They pray for others; they suffer for others; they labor for others; they offer themselves to Christ, therefore, for the Church present and future, for the faithful and for unbelievers, for the good and the wicked, for all children of God. Therefore, in a way, all children of a common Father are creditors of these most privileged ones.

The first born—that is, the first supernatural sons of St. Catherine of Siena and St. Thérèse of Lisieux were two criminals: two creatures abandoned by everyone, perhaps deserted by their natural mothers, and they were certainly unacquainted with any spiritual mothers. In the hour of their dejection and imprisonment, although the horror of universal condemnation covered them, they were loved as sons by St. Catherine and St. Thérèse, whose assistance was a pledge that Mary was near them. Standing beside one of these, and receiving his head into her hands, St. Catherine brought to him unknown peace and joy.

Virgin of virgins! Mother of virginity! Queen of the cloisters! Her image stirs the memory of motherhood and awakens the desire to be pure and virginal, whether we see her as a maiden at prayer with joined hands and face bent down in sweet abandonment to the Father; or whether we see her as the Mother with the Child of her womb sitting on her knee and contemplating Him with such infinite tenderness. Again we may find her standing in a niche in the cloister, or at the end of a corridor, or above the altar high amid a pyra-

mid of candles. Young men come to her, in the impetuosity of
their intellectual and physical vigor; old men, broken down
by trials or robust as oaks, come to her for courage and confidence.

The Madonna of love and of sorrow moderates the young,
tempering their exuberance with love, refining their harsh-
ness, and appeasing their resentments; while she uplifts the
old and downhearted with a gentle hand. Since she belongs
to all, she is Mother to all; making all aware of their brotherhood with one another, and pressing them about Christ, she
binds them closely together as brothers of Christ and of one
another.

The intellectual giant, the subtle theologian, the irresist-
ible orator are filled with a new sense of humility under the
gaze of her serene eyes. They no longer seek to extol themselves but to rest, to be sheltered like children under her
mantle, and thus their souls are made pure again, their intelligence takes on a virginal attitude, they find their way to
the Eternal, which was, perhaps, almost veiled by pride.

In the cells of their monasteries consecrated monks are not
alone; even if their own virility might bore them and make
them stern, the sincerity of the Mother renews them in grace.
Mary's smile brings warmth into cold cells and gives beauty
to bare walls. Her smiling countenance illumines hidden re-
cesses in the forests, enlivens mountain cloisters, and fills the
solitudes with enchantment. Thus she directs souls to her
Son and presents them to the Father; she espouses them to
the Holy Spirit.

Think of the poetry contained in the chivalrous election
by the Superior General of the Cistercian monks, of the Ma-
donna as their Lady Abbess. "In the house wherein the
Divine Mother is Abbess, Jesus works marvels." John of
Cirey used to say, "If by an absurd hypothesis, the devil and
Judas would observe the Cistercian rule with humility and

integrity, we would not despair of their final salvation, for the Virgin would succeed in saving them with her mercy." St. Albert the Great used to exclaim, "Often those whom the Son's justice would condemn, the Mother's mercy would set free." [21]

The old religious orders, contemplative or mendicant, were born and developed under Mary's protection, she being considered their Foundress or particular patroness. In reality, all virgins feel themselves children of Mary. In the East, St. John Damascene, Mary's flute player, asserted, "She is a Virgin and loves those who are virgins; she is chaste and loves the chaste. If we purify our imagination and our body, we shall constantly enjoy her favor." [22]

The Madonna and Woman

The highest honor of the feminine sex is in giving us Mary. Through Mary, as the Fathers of the Church explain, "the feminine sex is rehabilitated, annulling the sin of the first mother Eve." Mary is the model and beauty of maidens, the holiest of women and the flower of womanhood." [23]

> Hail Virgin, made a Mother;
> Happy Mother and unspoiled,
> The honor of every woman.[24]

"The sex that was first frail was first easily seduced," and "upon her breaks the strength of the evil one." [25]

The noblest task for a woman is to continue, in some

---

[21] "De Laudibus B.V.M.," II,1,23.
[22] *Op. cit.*, P.G. 96,752.
[23] A.H. 45,7, p. 27.
[24] "Ave, Virgo, mater facta,
  Mater felix et intacta,
  Decus omnis feminae." A.H. 54,227.
[25] A.H. 54, p. 251.

measure, Mary's mission among men. The Holy Family is the model of the Christian family and, in it, the woman should remind us of Mary. Mary is the Mother of mothers. While remaining a spotless Virgin, she became a unique Mother— a most perfect Mother.

The Christian family is also the Church in miniature; the father is, so to speak, like the priest, the mother is like the priestess. The family represents the Church, and Mary is the type of the Church. The trials of the Church are also the trials of the Christian family, and in the eyes of Christ can be offered up as such. The generation of children and their education is regarded as a participation in the work of the Creator: first, the formation of the physical life and then the development of the life of the soul.

The father is the head and the mother the foundation of the family; she waits upon all like the vestal priestess of the hearth. Her sons go out into the world with the father, but it is from her they go and to her they return. She guards and sustains the stability of the home amidst many cares; while with economy and labor she keeps, with resistance often heroic, the treasures of affection. The pressure of life all around tends to break down this family unity. This attempt is unceasing and sometimes one of her loved ones yields and leaves home. Then the mother quickly rises up in defense, to resist these inroads on family solidarity. It is she who, at every threat of danger, stops at nothing to restore family union. In her heart all live as one.

Outside the home, men and their modern daughters receive honors that in reality are more often injuries and delusions. The mother, hidden and selfless, follows and sustains them. At every turn and in every way she refreshes them from her own inexhaustible strength. Husband and sons may be leaders and men of business, philosophers or artists, political bosses of people, masters of technique, manual laborers, emigrants hardened by racial clashes, farmers hardened by the unyielding earth, but when they come into the radius of her influence, they fall into her arms, drop their shallow power, rise up from their humble status to find in her the sympathy that consoles them in their loneliness. She comforts them in the fears of life's night as she did when they were little ones.

Manhood fights and often gets angry, the woman—the mother—shelters mankind in her arms. She is like the Virgin Mother who holds on her lap and in her arms the Body of her Son, the Body she brought into the world. His followers had dispersed and gone away. His rich protectors Nicodemus and Joseph of Arimathea were in hiding, and in the general desertion only the faithful Mother remained, giving her last tribute of tears.

When death strips a home, as the wind strips a tree of its leaves, the mother stays on, the guardian of memories and family traditions, still resisting the action of time. She speaks of those who have gone as though they were present; she praises them as if they were still living and growing in age. Other women of the home, sisters and daughters, are also prototypes of Mary.

At times an impression is felt that religion might have been lost at least for a time, except for women. Christ might be lost to sight as when He was laid in the grave. There were only women then to watch His lifeless Body in its rocky tomb. The men were far away hiding behind their fears and their doubts, and feeling very fatigued.

It is often thus in homes. The husband becomes a prey to worry about provision for the family, dissipates his mind by frivolous literature and hides behind a false gaiety, while the sons amuse themselves by running after silly girls. It is lucky for the boys, if at home faithful wives, pure sisters, and anxious mothers pray, and repeat, almost timidly but patiently and insistently, a good word that reawakens, amidst the bitter revelry of vain things, some remembrance of those eternal truths—the soul, hell, judgment and the Virgin Mary. Those words are like open spaces through which comes the breath of life; they open into regions of light; they bring to us a pure air to clear the choking atmosphere of the world's foul places. All this, too, comes from Mary's activity.

Christ shed His Blood for the salvation of all men without exception. In order that each might be saved, He placed before Divine Justice an infinite price—His Precious Blood. But in the debt of love we owe the Father, is included the debt of love towards our brethren. The more love we give them, the more good we will do in their service; and so much the more shall we rejoice the Father since service done to the least of our brethren is a service rendered to Christ, the first born of our brethren.

In a word, we are saved, each in himself and each in all. Therefore in the Church we realize the Kingdom of God through union, collaboration, and in sharing responsibility with our brothers. With brothers and sisters: not just brothers with brothers and sisters with sisters only. In the Church all live together; and in the Church there is that universality described by St. Paul, which alone is of value, "there is no more Greek or barbarian, male or female, etc."

Since we are men, and human nature is an essential part of us in our time of trial in the world, this nature participates in, and becomes an essential factor in working out our trial. We bring to our testing the aptitudes of our human nature, so women contribute to the treasury of the Church, to the common sanctity, and in the Communion of Saints; they give especially those gifts of purity and love; while men bring, above all, their contribution of intelligence and strength. I say, *above all,* in a certain degree; because men also must be pure and must love; but women must understand well the reason for their faith, and work for the Kingdom of God.

In short, holy wives, sisters pure as virgins consecrated to God, are in the midst of the muddy flood of wantonness and avarice like so many filters of purification. When men return home, out of the by-ways of lust and contacts with the less clean, they wish to find in the mother, in the wife, in the sister, a look of innocence, hearts unhardened by cold calculating, souls that have not bartered God for some petty pleasure. And the great family of humanity expects to find in the cloisters of nuns and the convents of Sisters great reservoirs of purity, where is sung the poetry of spiritual life: mothers and sisters in grace, to whom can be entrusted the souls of children, of old people, of suffering people, to be reformed and reconstructed spiritually. When we enter the radius of religious women, we wish to breathe purity, to breathe Mary.

Since the greatest riches women can bring to the treasury of man's salvation—common to both men and women— consists in purity and love, then it is incumbent upon men to guard that purity and power for love which is inherent in their sisters, rather than frivolously attacking the one and profaning the other for a small gain. Lowering woman by making her a stupid plaything to be broken (with which also to break oneself) is to smash a masterpiece of God. When we read of the praise St. Ambrose, St. John Chrysostem, St. Basil bestowed upon their sisters, mothers and grandmothers, when we remember what St. Monica meant to St. Augustine, St. Scholastica meant to St. Benedict, St. Clotilde to St. Clovis, Aleth to St. Bernard; when we see in poetry the names of angels given to women, we can understand the great honor bestowed on souls made forever precious by the hand of the Creator and the Blood of the Redeemer; in the midst of the ordinary duties of life they acted with disinterestedness, purity and in a tenderness that resembled the angels.

Dante symbolized woman, formed by Christianity, in Beatrice, in Lucy, in Piccarda, creatures, who like Mary send everyone to Jesus; who are fountains of poetry, generators of joy, and, at the same time, channels of grace. "Mary of Vésins," said a Jocist leader about an associate, "has been for me all that she wanted to be—a little channel for Christ." [26] That is, a feeble model of Mary.

On the other hand, man does harm to himself, as well as to his sisters, when he wastes with stupid cunning the human and divine treasures in a woman; and those who lend themselves to this lowering of womanhood to that of a mere female, sell her immortal divinity for a few grimaces and a bit of bright tinsel. Woman falls from the status of angels to that of night birds and of the bats.

The defense of a woman, as also her garment of beauty, is her modesty. If she once renounces that, or she de-natures herself, she may think she is free and has achieved more joy in her existence, but in a short time all is dissolved before ever the first wrinkle has appeared on her face. Woman is revered when she is chaste; virtue will place under her feet a pedestal of sapphire. In the other case, what seems to be reverence is a caricature which, with the passing of years, appears as only sheer contempt, a figure of speech for poets of adventure and hunters of the contraband.

The woman who renounces virtue renounces her strength and her beauty. She degrades herself and falls into the power of the male sex whose slave she becomes although she may look adorned with jewels; as in fact she is, in the refined paganism of today, no less than she was in the less rational paganism of antiquity. Morality is the first greatness of women: Baptism, the other Sacraments, the Blood of Christ, the influence of the Virgin, which clothes her with such dignity that every attempt to rob her of it, or to violate her, is an attempt to destroy the Redemption of Christ. A man will

---

[26] "Mary of Vésins," "La Vie Intellectualle," 1914–1939. The Jocists are the associates of J.O.C. (Catholic Working Youth in France).

not pronounce a profane word or entertain an impure thought before a true and complete woman. She is one who enlightens souls by her sincere and pure countenance. Such was Mary; such was St. Catherine of Siena, St. Gemma Galgani and others.

In the middle of the second century, the rough Ermas, a freed slave redeemed by Baptism, said that a man, in order to overcome concupiscence had only to think of his own wife. He had in mind not the image of Venus but of his wife, the feeble copy of Mary, the woman holding the place of the Madonna. Once an American student, no doubt ignorant of Ermas' idea, answering a questionnaire on ways and means of overcoming temptations against purity, asserted, "I think of the Blessed Virgin and of the woman I was privileged to meet through her." [27]

ENEMIES OF THE VIRGIN

A perpetual enmity exists between Mary and the Prince of Evil—the destroyer of men. Since Mary never wearies of neutralizing the forces of evil, Satan gets his revenge as best he can by defaming the Virgin of her virginity and denying the Mother her motherhood. Therefore, if Mary is the one most loved of all creatures, she is also the one most readily hated. When a man, under the bewildering suggestion of the Evil One plots, or commits an ignoble act, and especially against purity, he first suppresses in his heart the thought of the WOMAN, Mary. His guilty feelings will cause him to blaspheme her. Her name is always like a barricade, opposing his entrance to houses of evil and, therefore, her name is cursed on the very threshold to free the way. When darkness is sought, the light of Mary is extinguished.

"O holy Mary, who dost illumine the whole world, pray

---

[27] Cf. "Studies." S. IV, p. 52, 1940.

13. *Nazareth*

for us!" So St. Bonaventure prayed, for this world is a vale of tears over which Mary bends like a mother in continual pain. It is not an act of chivalry that placed Mary at the summit of the human hierarchy, in which the past and future converge towards the Cross, rather, chivalry was a *consequence* of this.

It is because Mary was chosen by the Creator as the extraordinary means for bringing the divine into contact with the human. Philosophers are confounded in their efforts to achieve any other relationship between God and man; the gnostics invented a complicated system of beings, freeing themselves from the Unique Being by twos and by scores. The Creator needed not such complicated artifices, but with Divine simplicity took a simple girl from an ordinary village and associated her in an extraordinary act whose results have had such immense proportions. From all eternity the eye of God has scrutinized the hearts of millions of human beings and He chose this particular humble maiden because He found her more worthy than any other. For this reason He invested her with grace.

Nor does this fit in with the often erroneous judgments of human superficiality, which does not easily understand how the greatest of beings could wear the poorest of garments, and live in a discredited village

THE MONTH OF MAY

As soon as people take their stand for or against Jesus, they take their stand for or against His Mother. The discussions at the Council at Nice were followed by others that culminated in the Council of Ephesus. Every time men tried to cut away some vital part of Christianity, they attacked the divinity of Christ or the Motherhood of Mary.

Nor does heresy and hatred attack the Virgin Mary because of any special aversion for the highly privileged and yet lowly Israelite woman who saw her Son taken from her, first to give Himself for love of men and to abandon Himself to their leaders; seldom is any personal hatred manifested for her, but a deep aversion attacks her function as *Mother:* that Motherhood that warms and vivifies souls and, directed towards Christians as sons, completes the Christian family, giving it a sense of her love and filling Christian homes with the light of her smile.

Hatred attacks the very function that completes the family. On account of that Motherhood, hatred attacks the Church; which gathered around the Eucharist as around a hearth, transforming the world itself into the Church. Since there, Mary is the Mother, men are no longer orphans, and if they have reason to fear God the Father, and in their lowliness feel themselves far from their Creator, they can turn to her, who in her goodness shortens the distance, softens severity and, in a word, does all that a mother could not help doing.

The heresy that reduces or suppresses this action of Mary's motherly and moral mediation, is like taking away a pillar upon which a house stands; or like pulling down the main wall of the house, letting half the house fall and the other half remain suspended in space. The house is then open to hurricanes and storms. "Where Mary is missing," said a good Lutheran pastor, "one dies of cold."

In other words, if we cast out the Mother, the children are left orphans in all truth; it is impossible to think that the Son, her Spouse the Holy Ghost, and the Father, the Divine Trinity, Who performed such a miracle of Creation, could remain in a house from whence the Mother, the Spouse and the Daughter has been banished.

Now, heresy, knowingly or not, has aimed at this: to minimize man, destroy his dignity, and break his strength. The *virus* of this theological error explodes in the field of social action, and there works disorder. When heresy denies the light of reason, freedom of will, and moral responsibility in man, it only pretends to extol God; in reality, it seeks to demean His creature, lower man to the underground level; and the underground regions are the abode of Satan.

When heresy denies man this Mother, it robs him of his revivifying source of help in the continual mediating power of Mary, the sum of all his hopes upon which poetry shines. Man when orphaned, even if only of the mother, is more easily dominated; he is made weaker by the loss of a large fraction of his resistance, and thus falls a prey to Satan, his adversary and the prince of death.

In defending all of Mary's attributes, Catholics defend themselves; moreover, they defend the honor and patrimony of the Christian family. They prevent love and poetry from deserting that social unity where each one consummates in pain the laborious experience of life. They prevent the home and family life from disintegrating into cellular egoism.

Heretics cast out the Madonna and the Sisters, because both awake a love for the Father, motherly love, sisterly gentleness, and all those influences that seem soft to the promoters of material power and force. In the hearts of these modern tyrants there lurks an ancestral idolatry of monstrous myths, recognized by their ugliness, and placed over a mob to terrorize it like jailers in a concentration camp. The gentleness of the Sisters seems to weaken the system which reduces the human family to the status of a herd, used only for carrying materials in the construction of some gigantic work, under the whip of supervisors whose hearts are empty of all human feelings.

That smile from a kind heart, like an opalescence of light that brightens the gloom of the jail, that look of meek resignation, the sympathetic touch of pure hands caressing the hands of little children and washing ulcerated wounds, are neutralizing their cruel effort; it is human kindness returning to inhumanity; it is a breath from heaven entering the underground mazes. Therefore the dictators opposed it. Where the Mother is, there are no slaves, but sons. We must not exploit our neighbor, because he is a brother. We must not bleed others, but we must give ourselves, even in sacrifice.

Where Mary goes, she draws after her beauty and the might of the Gospel, like a train of stars. Where she is, her Son is also, in Whom men are brothers because she was given to them as a Mother. Where this Mother is, likewise all mothers both by grace and by nature, plus the Sisters, it would not be easy to start a war; because to faces dark with hatred are opposed their pleading faces and tearful eyes; and of those who seek blood, they ask for pity.

MARY THE MEDIATRIX

In a vision, St. Gertrude saw under Mary's mantle, tigers, lions and other wild animals, symbols of sinners, because the Mother's protection extends to all her sons, even the sinful ones. Grace elevates nature but grace does not destroy it; grace divinizes nature but does not render it less human. What happens according to nature? When children want some favor from the father, or fear his anger, they turn to their mother. The circuit runs thus: sons go to the mother,

the mother goes to the father. In a sense it is the way of generating in reverse. The same is true in the supernatural order.

Mary's sons, the redeemed, aware of their weakness and
their faults, turn to God by way of their Mother; they go to
the Father through her. Mary, our Mother, is our go-between.
That is her perpetual function as Mother of grace. We really
return to God the way the Word came to us, but in reverse.
The Word was united to our flesh through Mary. Humanity
did not deserve to be united to God on account of Original
Sin. God made use of a unique person in this world, the Immaculate Virgin, by whom tainted flesh was cleansed; even
to offering it to the Word that He might be Incarnate.

The requests we make to God become oblations when presented by her pure hands; the hands of Mary purify them.
They reach Jesus in the same way as He came to us. St. Bernard says, "Her hands are lilies shining with whiteness, and
God, the friend of lilies, will not be displeased with an offering placed in Mary's hands among lilies."

Flesh, that is to say, humanity, was united to Christ through
Mary, and was redeemed by Christ through His Blood
formed in Mary's bosom. The union of God with man was
effected in Mary's womb; it continues to take place in Mary's
heart. Jesus is the unique, eternal Mediator between the
Father and men. Mary is still the way between Christ and
humanity, uniting the two. "As our advocate, she is near the
Son, as the Son is near the Father; or rather, she pleads our
cause and places our petitions before the Father and the
Son." [28]

"The Lord was with her and she was with the Father of
mercy in working out our salvation. . . ." [29] Therefore, she
is the Co-Redemptrix, and channel of graces. She offered the
Saviour to the world; she continues to offer salvation in Him.

---

[28] St. Albert the Great, "De Laudibus B.V.M." II,17.
[29] *Idem.* I,4.

If Jesus is the new Adam, Mary is the new Eve. As the first mother Eve had been given to the first father, Adam, for a companion and helpmate, so the new Mother Mary is given by God to Christ as companion and helper in the work of Redemption, which is unceasing. It was she who conceived our universal Redeemer, Christ.

She remains a mother towards Christ with the eternal rights of a divine motherhood, which therefore is eternal. She remains the one who obtained the miracle of water changed into wine and who rejoices in seeing that wine changed into His Precious Blood; she is Mother of the Eucharist and promoter of the miracle.

She, more than any other creature, suffered with Christ and for Christ in His Crucifixion; meriting then and throughout her whole life, *de congruo*, according to the expressing of theologians; that is, by fitness, what Christ had merited *de condigno*—by justice. The Blood of the Son gave a condign value to the Mother's tears. Our souls live by that value. Finally, Mary co-operated with God in time in the redeeming of humanity, and continues to co-operate in eternity: "regenerator of fallen humanity, most powerful Mediatrix for the whole world and consequently, the dispenser of all the riches that Jesus has won for us by His Blood and His death." [30]

In a word, "God has willed that we should receive all through Mary." All this is clear to love and obvious to reason, for Jesus is the beginning of all things, cause and form of the universe, the plasma of holiness. Mary is His Mother, and therefore what comes to us from Jesus comes to us also from her. He is as much the Son of the Eternal Father as He is the Son of the Virgin Mother; He loves the one and the other infinitely. For this love, there is no desire of Mary that He will not grant.

---

[30] Pius X. Encycl., *"ad diem illum."* Feb. 2, 1904.

So mighty art thou, Lady, and so great,
That he who grace desireth, and cometh not
To Thee for aidence, fain would have
Desire fly without wings.[31]

And Mary as the Mother of Christ is our Mother. Christ is our Brother because we have her in common with Him as our Mother. And she is also the new Eve. If the old Eve was the universal mediatrix of guilt, the new Eve is the universal Mediatrix of grace.

Christ is the Fount of Grace, the gift by which God sanctifies us and makes us capable of enjoying Him in eternal beatitude; but Mary is the dispenser of this life-giving gift. Christ is the Head of the Church, and His gifts are communicated to the Church by way of Mary, who is, in His Mystical Body, what the neck is in our physical bodies. The neck joins the head to the rest of the body for all communications. These images and figures are used by the Saints and by popes. And they call Mary, inasmuch as she is the conveyor of salvation, "the vein of the Trinity," to Whom she is bound by a threefold tie.

Redemption goes on, and the Church goes on, and the action of Mary as Mother of grace continues. Her motherhood continues in the generation and growth of believers whose lives gradually complete the whole Body of Christ, her Son.

Such mediation, such distribution of the Son's graces by the hands of the Mother is a natural outcome. A courtesy given by a gentlewoman, an act of charity done with the smile of a sister or mother, grows in value. Graces are from God, but it pleases Him—and therefore pleases us too—to distribute them by the hands of His fair Lady. Thus is she honored.

---

[31] Dante, Par. 33: 13–15.

Her honor gladdens the hearts of men and by it He is pleased Who from eternity was pleased with Mary.

Mary is indispensable in divinizing man, as she was indispensable in the Incarnation of God. Mary was "invented" by God to bring God down to men and to bring men to God; it is this that constitutes her the distributor of all graces for all creatures.

She is the heart of the Church and she gathers all things for her Son: she collects and keeps, like every good and intelligent mother, especially like the mother of such a privileged and only Son. She gathers for Him. What she does and causes others to do, is for Him, to Whom she brings the affections of all as well as her own, since she lives in Him and for Him. Therefore, the devotion, the love, and poetry of which she is the source, express only one unvaried, pure solicitation to bring souls back to Him; as the theologians say, "We go to Jesus through Mary:" *ad Jesum per Mariam;* by a path of lilies and roses.

DAUGHTERS OF ST. PAUL

IN MASSACHUSETTS
   50 St. Paul's Ave.
   Jamaica Plain
   Boston, Mass. 02130
   172 Tremont St.
   Boston, Mass. 02111
   381 Dorchester St.
   So. Boston, Mass. 02127
   325 Main St.
   Fitchburg, Mass.
IN NEW YORK
   78 Fort Place
   Staten Island, N.Y. 10301
   625 East 187th St.
   Bronx, N.Y.
   39 Erie St.
   Buffalo, N.Y. 14202
IN CONNECTICUT
   202 Fairfield Ave.
   Bridgeport, Conn. 06603
IN OHIO
   141 West Rayen Ave.
   Youngstown, Ohio 44503
   Daughters of St. Paul
   Cleveland, Ohio
IN TEXAS
   114 East Main Plaza
   San Antonio, Texas 78205
IN CALIFORNIA
   1570 Fifth Ave.
   San Diego, Calif. 92101
   278 - 17th Street
   Oakland, California 04012
IN LOUISIANA
   86 Bolton Ave,
   Alexandria, La. 71303
IN FLORIDA
   2700 Biscayne Blvd.
   Miami, Florida 33137
IN CANADA
   8885 Blvd. Lacordaire
   St. Leonard Deport-Maurice
   Montreal Canada
     1063 St. Clair Ave. West
   Toronto Canada
IN ENGLAND
   20 Beauchamp Place
   London, S.W. 3, England
IN AFRICA
   Box 4392
   Kampala, Uganda
IN INDIA
   Water Field Road Extension
   Plot No. 143
   Bandra, India
IN THE PHILIPPINE ISLANDS
   2650 F.B. Harrison St.
   Pasay City
   Philippine Islands
IN AUSTRALIA
   58 Abbotsford Rd.
   Homebush N S.W., Australia
   226 Victoria Square
   Adelaide, South-Australia
   6 Muir Street
   Hawthorn, Victoria, Australia